Seeking Sukha

A Journey to Self Mastery and Lasting Happiness

By Duncan Starr-Boltt

May you achieve everything you desire in life, to feel good

Contents

Acknowledgements

First and foremost, I would like to acknowledge the profound wisdom of the yogis and Buddhists who have dedicated their lives to self-mastery. They are true inspirations, showing us that inner peace is not just possible but attainable. Without their example, how could we know such peace exists and be drawn to follow this path ourselves?

I am indebted to Sadhguru and Isha Foundation for the huge breakthroughs in my own life. While volunteering for Isha, they taught me how to "enjoy washing each dish" and were my inspiration for the monks tasks. Sadhguru's clarity of thinking continues to inspire me as I develop on this path.

Special thanks to Swami ji and his school in Rishikesh, "Yoga Essence". The four days of silence there became a pivotal part for this book. The laughter we shared still brings a smile to my heart and tears to my eyes. To all the amazing students I shared this experience with—thank you.

I am deeply grateful to Thich Nhat Hanh for his teachings on the Buddha, for his insights and wisdom. He stands as a shining example of happiness and peace despite experiencing incredible hardship in his own life.

To my family—you have each shaped who I am:

To my mother, thank you for showing me what true love feels like and being a shining example of happiness and optimism, seeing the good in everyone you meet.

To my step-father Andrew, thank you for teaching me morals and generosity, and for being our rock through all life's challenges.

To my dad, thank you for always being excited to hear about my ambitious plans to change the world, and for helping shape my understanding of the mind through our countless conversations.

Finally, and most importantly, to my wife Gill—thank you for being my partner in all these adventures. Your support in letting me travel to India for a month alone, and your willingness to embrace our dream of living in Crete, shows a rare courage and trust. You are not just my life partner but my companion on this journey of growth and discovery. This book, like all our adventures, is as much yours as it is mine.

Your combined influence has made this work possible.

Chapter One

Is this Really Success?

The vast hall at ExCeL London buzzed with energy, the kind of electric anticipation that came with the promise of transformation. Thousands of attendees sat in neat rows, their eyes fixed on the stage. Spotlights swept the crowd, illuminating eager faces, notebooks open, pens poised.

The International Conference on Success and Motivation was the pinnacle of its kind, a glittering showcase of the world's most celebrated thinkers, doers, and achievers.

And at the very top of the marquee: him—Harrison Marshall.

He stepped into the light, the roar of applause washing over him. It was a sound he'd once found intoxicating, the ultimate affirmation of his work and worth. But tonight, it felt hollow, like an echo in an empty room. He adjusted the mic clipped to his tailored jacket and smiled, the polished grin he'd perfected over years of speaking tours.

For all his success, he couldn't remember the last time he'd felt truly happy.

The thought surfaced unbidden, tugging at the edges of his focus. He glanced at the massive screen behind him, where his name, "The Success Architect," was emblazoned in bold letters, a title he had worn with pride. Now it felt like a costume, a role he was struggling to believe in.

"What is success?"

His voice carried effortlessly through the hall, practised and resonant. He had asked this question a thousand times before. It was the hook, the opening line that always drew them in. But tonight, as he posed it, the words felt weightless, untethered to meaning.

"For some, success is wealth," he continued, pacing slowly across the stage. "For others, it's achieving a dream, climbing the corporate ladder, running a business, or creating something that lasts. Success is as unique as the individual striving for it."

The audience nodded along, captivated. He had their attention, as always. Yet, as he spoke, a whisper of doubt gnawed at him: Success should involve happiness, shouldn't it?

He delivered his lines with the precision of a craftsman, each anecdote and insight designed to inspire, to uplift. But a deeper truth stirred beneath the surface. He had spent years selling the dream of success—books, workshops, coaching sessions, all promising the keys to a better life. Yet, too often, he'd watched his clients, now good friends, burn out, break down, or become disillusioned.

And now, he felt the same cracks forming within himself.

As the applause thundered again, he felt the familiar rush, the fleeting euphoria that came from standing in front of thousands and being adored. But he knew what awaited him after this: the crash.

The emails and messages were endless, the phone calls incessant. Each success brought a fleeting high but left behind a growing void. Even the weekends, spent unwinding with friends over drinks, felt like shallow distractions from a deeper ache. He loved the applause, the rush of wealth, the sense of accomplishment—but it no longer felt like enough.

Backstage, the energy shifted. Staff buzzed around him, congratulating him on another stellar performance. A junior assistant handed him a glass of water and a schedule for the next day's events. But their words barely registered.

He retreated to the green room, the door clicking shut behind him. Alone, he sank into a chair, staring at his reflection in the mirror. His tailored suit, his perfect hair, the faint glimmer of sweat on his brow—it all looked immaculate. Polished. Successful.

But beneath the surface, his mind raced. The exhaustion he'd pushed aside now crashed over him like a wave. He wanted to sleep, to let go of the noise in his head. Instead, his phone buzzed again. Another email. Another demand. He turned it face down on the table, but the constant pull of checking and replying still gnawed at him.

That night, he crashed into bed, the adrenaline of the evening's performance still coursing through his veins. His body was heavy with exhaustion, but his mind wouldn't quiet. He tossed and turned, trying to find a comfortable position, but sleep evaded him.

At some point he did finally drift off, but it wasn't long before he woke again, jolted by a rush of excitement mixed with anxiety.

Thoughts of the conference, his clients, his unfinished projects, and the growing question of his own happiness swirled together. He sat up, staring at the faint glow of his phone on the nightstand.

The urge to check it was overwhelming. What emails had come in? How many likes had his latest post received? Who needed him? The pull was irresistible, and with a sigh, he reached for the phone, scrolling mindlessly in the dark.

For a fleeting moment, the distraction felt good. But as the minutes turned to hours, he felt hollow again. The excitement had shifted to restlessness, then to frustration. He lay back down, staring at the ceiling, his heart still racing.

Why can't I just feel at peace? he thought. He had everything—success, wealth, admiration—but he still craved more, why did it all feel so empty?

This had become a nightly ritual and a growing concern. He felt like such a fraud. He couldn't even sleep, recover, and relax. He knew sleep was so important to stave off the burnout and breakdowns that had caught so many of his clients.

Chapter Two

A Teacher Finds You

Morning arrived, but it brought no relief. Harrison felt more tired than when he'd gone to bed. As he stood in front of the mirror, the polished image from the night before seemed faded, worn at the edges. His suit jacket, draped over the chair, felt like an old disguise. The question returned, louder this time: There must be another way?

The thought lingered as he packed his bag for the day. Answers—he needed something. Anything. He grabbed his coat and set out for his usual morning walk, a small ritual he clung to for some semblance of balance in his life.

The park greeted him like an old friend, its gates opening onto a sanctuary of green amidst the city's restless pulse. He had always found solace here, a fleeting sense of ease under the canopy of towering trees. Majestic oaks stood like ancient guardians, their gnarled branches reaching skyward. Towering pines released a faint, earthy aroma that mingled with the dew-soaked grass.

In the heart of the park lay a tranquil lake, its glassy surface reflecting the pale morning sky. Ducks glided effortlessly across the water, and a lone swan moved with quiet grace. Near the far end, a small stone pavilion stood beneath a canopy of wisteria vines, its archways framing glimpses of the city skyline beyond.

A modest shrine nearby added a spiritual stillness to the air, where saffron-robed monks gathered daily, their presence adding to the park's quiet reverence.

Harrison found a bench near the lake and sank into it, letting out a long breath. The city skyline loomed in the distance—a reminder of deadlines, meetings, and obligations—but here, it felt softened, almost surreal. The air was crisp and clean, carrying the faint scent of blooming flowers and damp earth. For a moment, the world seemed unusually still, yet inside him, chaos brewed.

He tapped his foot restlessly against the gravel path, adjusted his phone in his pocket, and fought the familiar itch to pull it out. Normally, this park brought him peace. Normally, the sound of leaves rustling in the breeze and the distant chatter of birds would soothe him. But today, his mind raced ahead to the hours waiting for him—the emails, the calls, the empty promises he had to keep. He stared at the lake, his reflection distorted in the ripples, feeling utterly drained.

I need help, he thought, a pang of shame hitting him. But where do I even begin?

Lost in thought, he barely noticed someone sit down at the far end of the bench. The figure was quiet, still. After a few moments, a calm, warm voice broke the silence.

"You seem troubled."

Harrison looked up, startled. At the end of the bench sat a monk dressed in simple robes, his hands resting easily on his lap. The monk smiled warmly.

"Yes, it's been a tough week," Harrison said hesitantly, reluctant to admit his failures.

"I see... you have a hard life?" the monk said, chuckling. His tone was playful but firm. The statement surprised Harrison, and he returned the warm smile.

Harrison studied the monk for a moment, noticing his serene expression. Despite the simplicity of his appearance, there was a quiet confidence in the way he sat, as if the weight of the world didn't touch him.

"You're right," Harrison said. "I have a great life. Everything I've ever wanted. But I feel worse than ever." He paused. "You seem happy. How is that possible? I mean, really happy?"

The monk smiled gently, his eyes filled with genuine kindness. "Yes. Contentment is a constant background to my life. There is no chase for me, no ups and downs. I enjoy the flow of life as it comes."

Harrison leaned forward, intrigued but sceptical. "How? Everyone I know is either chasing something or recovering from something. Even when things are good, it doesn't last."

The monk's gaze softened, and he replied with great care. "You live a life of desires. Your whole day revolves around seeking happiness in the pursuit of objects—success, recognition, possessions—which you imagine will bring you fulfilment." He paused, then added firmly, "Desire should be abandoned not because it is evil, but because it is the root of suffering."

The words struck Harrison like a lightning bolt. He blinked, leaning back into the bench as the truth of the statement settled into his mind.

"That makes sense. But—" He paused, grappling with the thought. "When I desire something, it gives me so much energy, so much drive. And when I achieve it, I feel so good. How can I just let go of that?"

The monk watched him closely, noticing his restless movements. Harrison shifted his position again, adjusted his shirt, and reached into his pocket to check for his phone, even though it hadn't buzzed.

The monk gestured gently to Harrison's hands. "The search for the spiritual path is born out of suffering, and it seems you are finally ready. So I will answer this when you can sit."

Harrison frowned, confused. He looked down at himself. "But I am sitting right now."

The monk's eyes twinkled with a hint of humour. "No. Right now, you are in constant motion. You are on this bench, yes, but your body cannot be still. And until your body can be quiet, how can we hope to quiet your mind?"

Harrison saw the monk's point; he hadn't noticed his restlessness until now. "So... what do I do?"

The monk paused, his calm gaze meeting Harrison's eyes once more. "Your ability to flow with abundance is clear. The flow of life has brought you and me together, and if it's meant to, it will take you further."

Harrison thought about this. He understood something about flow—how success had come naturally to him when he was in the right state of mind, when everything seemed to align effortlessly. But he had never looked at it quite like this before.

"Do you mean I should just relax, and the solution will come to me naturally?"

The monk shook his head gently, a faint smile playing at his lips. "The flow of life isn't some mystical force; it's simply energy at play—a constant dance. But the human mind can't possibly comprehend the full complexity of the universe and how it moves. A good way to understand it is to break it down a little—to see it as a series of interconnected systems. Your body is a system of cells working in harmony. This park is a system of trees, plants, and animals. The city is a system of people, buildings, and transportation. This country is another system, and the world itself is a vast system of which you are one small, essential part—much like a single cell in your body."

The monk paused, letting his words settle before continuing. "When you pay attention, you can see how these systems flow. You can't just relax and expect to achieve your aim in life like the world will take care of it for you. You still need to put the work in, ask the right questions and respond to the right things, be involved, pay attention, and things will flow."

Harrison felt a familiar truth in these words. He had always worked this way—trusting his gut instincts, knowing who to work with and who to avoid, sensing opportunities that others overlooked. This skill had refined itself through years of experience. But now he realised something new: The flow had brought him here. It had brought him to this park, to this bench, to this conversation. If he hadn't asked the question that morning, if he hadn't been ready—truly ready—this meeting might have still happened, but it wouldn't have been the same.

A flicker of determination sparked in him. "So... can you teach me to sit?"

The monk's smile widened, and he gave a small nod of approval. "I could. But in this city, there are countless teachers who can guide you in sitting still. And for your first lesson, you must figure this out for yourself."

Harrison nodded in understanding.

"You will find your teacher, or they will find you," the monk said. "Pay attention. See the suffering in your desires and be ready to let them go."

The monk rose to his feet, his movements unhurried, deliberate, as though each step carried purpose. "My life is dedicated to helping people find peace. So if this is what you truly want, I'll see you again—when you can sit still."

Before Harrison could respond, the monk offered a broad, heartfelt smile. He bowed deeply, then turned and walked calmly across the park, his saffron robe catching the morning light. Harrison watched as the monk's figure grew smaller and smaller, finally disappearing near the shrine in the distance.

Left alone on the bench, Harrison looked down at his hands. They were fidgeting, his fingers tapping lightly against his knee. He glanced out at the city skyline, the towering buildings rising above the trees.

For the first time, he noticed the tightness in his chest, the tension in his shoulders—the restless hum of energy vibrating through his body. He shifted uncomfortably on the bench, realising something profound: He had no idea how to simply... be still.

The city buzzed on in the background, cars honking, people walking briskly to their destinations. Harrison sat there, staring at the lake, feeling the weight of the monk's words settle into his chest.

"When you can sit still."

It was such a simple instruction, yet it felt monumental. And as the cool morning breeze brushed against his face, Harrison closed his eyes briefly, breathing in deeply.

The journey had begun.

Chapter Three

The Journey Begins at Home

Harrison grabs his notepad out of his briefcase. The best way to learn anything for him has always been to write. It clarifies his thoughts, and allows him to condense the information down to consistent points he can remember. The notebook in front of him lay open, blank except for a few scribbled words: "The search for the spiritual path is born out of suffering."

He taps the pen against the bench, then stops himself—catching the restless habit. He sets the pen down deliberately and takes a deep breath.

"Okay," he murmurs to himself. "What did he say? Desire is the root of suffering, but it's not evil. It's just... what keeps us chasing."

He writes down the monk's words, then rewrites them in his own terms: "Happiness isn't in the chase? This is new. The highs and lows are the problem. I need to learn to sit still—physically first, then mentally. Trust the flow of life."

He pauses, staring at the page. The last point catches his attention.

Leaning back on the bench, he thinks about his life. Success has always come to him—almost effortlessly. Deals closing, people gravitating toward him, opportunities appearing at the right time. He's always thought of it as luck, or maybe his own hard work, but now the monk's words echo in his mind: "You have a natural flow."

He pulls out his laptop, curious, and searches for articles on "flow in life." He finds a mix of ideas:

- The psychology of flow states—how focus and alignment create effortless progress
- Philosophical ideas about life as a river, flowing naturally when you stop resisting
- Practical advice about making good decisions and trusting the process

"It's not magic," he thinks. "It's not some supernatural force. It's just... how life works. Do the right things, make the right choices, and life flows."

He feels a spark of excitement, like he's uncovered something deeply true. He writes down: "Flow isn't mystical—it's natural. It's about alignment and trusting yourself. I need to let life guide me to what's next."

The next step was clear. The monk said his body needs to be still before his mind can quiet. He stares at the notebook again, tapping his pen before catching himself once more.

"So, how do I learn to sit?" he muses. "I need a teacher, but he said to trust the flow. That means... I don't have to force it. Just live my life, pay attention, and see where the flow takes me."

He nods, feeling a sense of clarity. For the first time in a while, he feels calm—like he doesn't have to have all the answers right now.

He glances at the time. It's mid-morning, and the familiar pull of work tugs at him. He can't switch off completely—there's still an itch to be productive. He closes the notebook.

"Maybe I'll take a walk, grab a coffee, just pay attention and see what happens," he thinks. "But first..." He feels a natural pull towards his phone. "Let's check social media."

He gets out his phone for the first time in forty minutes, scrolling through his social feeds. The comments and likes on his latest post feel like a quick hit of adrenaline, but they're immediately followed by unease. He notices the patterns:

- The same cycle of validation and emptiness.
- Followers looking to him for answers he doesn't have.

He sets the phone down, realising he's tapping his foot again. A small laugh escapes him—it's a moment of self-awareness he wouldn't have had yesterday.

"Okay," he says to himself. "Let's not get stuck here. Walk first, work later."

Harrison walks through the park, his jacket zipped against the morning chill. At first, his thoughts are scattered, but as he moves, something shifts. His pace slows, his breath steadies, and his eyes begin to take in the world around him.

He notices things he's never paid attention to before:

- A group of businesspeople pacing in agitation, phones glued to their ears, their movements hurried and restless.
- A dog owner sitting on a bench, petting their calm, content dog—both seem at ease, the dog's head resting in the owner's lap.
- An older woman on a nearby bench, doing nothing except watching the world go by, her posture relaxed, her expression peaceful.

He walks further, thinking about the monk's calm, grounded presence. "What would the monk do?" he asks himself. The question feels surprisingly helpful, almost like a guiding hand.

He realises something: "Having someone to model... it makes all the difference. The monk inspires me. It's not just about being told what to do—it's about seeing how he lives, how he moves through life. I can choose better because I've seen better."

He feels a sense of gratitude toward the monk, even though the encounter was brief. He straightens his posture, smiles, and continues his walk.

As he approaches his favourite coffee shop, he sees the older woman he noticed earlier standing outside, basking in the sunshine. Her eyes are closed, a faint smile on her face.

For the first time in years, he doesn't rush past. Instead, he slows, holds the door open for her as she turns towards the coffee shop. She smiles warmly.

"Why, thank you, young man," she says.

He smiles back, feeling something unexpected, genuine pleasure.

"It's my pleasure," he replies. And for the first time in a long time, he means it.

Inside, the coffee shop hums with quiet conversation and the scent of fresh pastries. The old lady stands behind him in the queue. After a moment, she leans in, her voice kind.

"How are you, dear? Can I buy you a coffee?"

He shakes his head, smiling. "That's very kind, but no, thank you. I'm good. But actually, I noticed you sitting earlier—you seemed so... still. How do you do that?"

The old lady chuckles softly. "Oh, I just enjoy the sunshine. It's a gift, you know."

Harrison hesitates, then blurts out, "Could you teach me to sit with that kind of stillness?"

The old lady looks at him kindly but shakes her head. "Oh, no, dear. I'm no teacher. I wouldn't know where to start."

The conversation catches the ear of the young woman behind the counter. She's tall, with a calm, grounded energy that immediately strikes Harrison. Her movements are deliberate, her voice steady as she joins in.

"If you want to learn to sit still, have you tried yoga?" she asks. "I get so much stillness from it myself, and we really do learn to sit still."

Harrison blinks, intrigued. "Yoga?"

She nods, handing him his coffee along with a small, neatly folded leaflet. "My teacher is brilliant and has taught me so much. It's how I learnt to slow down and bring stillness into my life. Here's her information."

Harrison takes the leaflet, it feels like a gift. He glances at it: a name, an address, and a photo of a serene-looking woman seated in lotus pose.

"Thank you," he says.

The barista smiles as she turns to the man behind him.

There is a timetable on the back of the leaflet, and he notices there is a class in a few hours. He relaxes, impressed with how easily the answer the monk promised had come to him. But he also laughs at himself for not thinking of yoga, or at least some form of eastern teachings, sooner. No wonder the monk seemed so confident he would find a teacher. He relaxes and enjoys his coffee, then heads home to change.

Chapter Four

And Now Yoga

The studio's exterior is unassuming—just a small sign reading "Inner Path Yoga" above a simple glass door. Harrison hesitates outside, gripping the leaflet, before finally stepping inside.

The scent of sandalwood greets him, along with the gentle murmur of conversation. The space is warm and welcoming, with soft light filtering through gauzy curtains. A few people sit on mats, stretching or meditating, their movements deliberate and calm.

Behind the desk stands a woman with a serene smile, the same one from the leaflet. She greets him with a gentle nod.

"Welcome, I am Grace. You must be new," she says.

He feels slightly out of place—he really has never done anything like this before, and he worries he's disturbing them, but manages a smile.

"Yes, I'm a complete beginner," he admits. "I'm strong and fit but not very flexible i'm afraid."

Her smile widens. "That's how most people start. It's lovely to have you here."

She asks him to remove his shoes, guiding him into the studio to sit on a mat.

Harrison sits on his mat, surrounded by others of all ages and levels. He fidgets, adjusting his posture, struggling to sit still, but gradually starting to relax.

Grace's voice is calm but firm as she guides them into a simple standing posture, arms raised overhead.

He lifts his arms confidently, already familiar with the burn of physical exertion. But after a few breaths, his arms begin to ache in an unfamiliar way—not the clean burn of lifting weights, but a dull, nagging fatigue.

"Why does this hurt so much?" he thinks. "I bench press twice my body weight. This should be easy."

His shoulders tremble slightly. He grits his teeth, pushing through the discomfort, his competitive edge kicking in.

Grace's voice floats over the room. "Breathe slowly. Inhale deeply through the nose, exhale longer than you inhale. Let the breath guide you."

He tries, forcing the air in and out as instructed. But the slower he breathes, the harder it becomes. It feels like choking, like his lungs are rebelling against the deliberate slow pace.

"This is ridiculous. Just hold the pose," he thinks to himself.

He abandons the slow breathing, focusing entirely on the postures. The pain builds as they move into deeper stretches, but he welcomes it, using it as fuel to push harder. Sweat drips down his forehead, and his jaw tightens with the effort.

"Pain is weakness leaving the body. Keep going," he tells himself.

As the class progresses, he begins to notice something strange. His mind grows quieter. The usual storm of thoughts, work tasks, social media, endless to-do lists fades into the background. His focus narrows to the here and now: the stretch of his hamstrings, the tremble in his arms, the instructor's calm voice.

For the first time in years, he feels entirely in his body.

The class ends with shavasana—corpse pose. He lies flat on his back, arms at his sides, palms facing up. At first his mind resists the stillness. He fidgets slightly, adjusting his shoulders.

"Let go," Grace says. "The work is done. Just be."

The words settle into him like a weight. Slowly, his body melts into the mat. His breath evens out without effort, and his mind lets go.

When he opens his eyes, the room is brighter, and the other students are already gathering their mats. He blinks, momentarily disoriented, before realising he must have dozed off.

"I fell asleep?" he thinks. "How? I never fall asleep during the day."

But he feels incredible, refreshed, alive, his body humming with energy. The stiffness in his shoulders is gone, replaced by a sense of looseness and strength. His mind, usually a chaotic whirl, feels... calm.

As he rolls up his mat, he approaches Grace. "That was great, thank you. I feel so much better. Maybe I'll do some more when I get home."

She shakes her head, her expression kind but firm. "Your body needs time to adjust. Yoga is new for you—start slowly. Relax, you have done enough today."

He nods, thinking about how challenging the class had been. He furrows his brow, used to pushing through physical limits every day. But something about her calm authority makes him pause.

As he walks home, he feels his body moving differently. His stride is smoother, his shoulders relaxed. For once, he's not thinking about work or social media, he's simply enjoying the walk.

The monk's words echo in his mind: "Stillness begins with the body."

He stops at a bench to jot a note in his journal, the idea crystallising in his mind: "Stillness begins with the body. It makes sense—how can the mind rest if the body is always in motion?"

He adds another line: "I've never felt so refreshed, so calm. I've spent years chasing highs and fighting through stress, but this—this is something different."

Back home, Harrison feels a lightness he hasn't experienced in years. His body feels alive—loose, strong, and refreshed. His breathing has slowed naturally, and his mind feels calm. Inspired by the monk's words and his newfound stillness, he decides to try sitting.

He sets up on the floor, crossing his legs with determination. But almost immediately, the reality of his body catches up with him. His knees ache, his lower back rounds forward, and he struggles to hold himself upright.

"How is this so hard?" he thinks. "I'm fit. I'm strong."

He props himself against the wall, finding some relief. Closing his eyes, he tries to recapture the peace he had felt in the yoga class. But the discomfort creeps in, sharp pressure in his knees, a dull ache in his back. Frustration bubbles up.

With a groan, he straightens his legs, leaning back on his hands. The relief is immediate but tinged with disappointment.

"I thought I was healthy," he reflects. "Turns out, I have a long way to go."

For a moment he feels defeated. But then, a flicker of determination: "This is just the beginning."

He heads to the kitchen and brews himself a coffee. The familiar routine calms him, the smell of freshly ground beans, the hiss of the espresso machine. Holding the mug in both hands, he takes a slow sip, savouring the rich taste and warmth.

Sitting at the table, he feels present in a way he hasn't in years. Coffee has always been a small joy in his life, a ritual that brings him into the moment. He smiles to himself.

"This is progress," he thinks. "I haven't checked my phone all afternoon."

A quick glance at the clock reveals it's 3 PM. He blinks in surprise. "The longest I've gone without my phone in years." The realisation fills him with pride.

Inspired, he decides to share his experience. Opening his phone, he writes a post about his first yoga class and the surprising impact it had on him. He hesitates for a moment—this is a big shift from his usual high-energy, success-driven posts. But something inside pushes him forward. He hits "Post" and waits.

Minutes tick by., no likes, no comments. He starts to feel hollow, second-guessing himself.

"What was I thinking?" he wonders. "One yoga class and I'm already posting about it? People probably think I've lost it."

His hand starts to shake, an old nervous habit, and he paces the room. Refreshing the post again and again, he considers deleting it.

Then, suddenly: 52 likes.

Relief floods him. He exhales, sinking into a chair as notifications start pouring in. Comments fill the screen—people praising yoga, sharing their own experiences, and recommending teachers.

"Wow," he thinks. "I had no idea so many people already do yoga."

He dives into the comments, responding to followers, liking their suggestions, and feeling a growing connection. It's exhilarating, this sense of engagement and validation.

Ninety minutes pass before he realises how absorbed he's been. The likes have climbed to over 200, and the comments keep coming. His followers are engaged, sharing their stories and thanking him for his openness. He feels validated, even inspired.

As the night wears on, he gets more and more involved. Responding to comments turns into liking other posts, which turns into scrolling his feed. He feels connected, energised—on fire, even. His mind races with ideas for his next post.

When he finally glances at the time, it's almost midnight. He knows he should wind down, but the energy coursing through him won't let him. He makes another coffee, rationalising it as a way to brainstorm.

By the time he finally gets into bed, his heart is racing. He lies still for a few minutes, eyes closed, but his thoughts are too loud—the buzz of likes, comments, and his growing audience fill his mind.

He rolls over, grabs his phone, and checks his post again. The likes have passed 800. A grin spreads across his face.

"This is incredible," he thinks. "People are loving it."

But when he puts the phone down, he's too wired to sleep. The coffee, the excitement, the constant engagement—it's all too much. His breathing is shallow, his heart thudding in his chest. After an hour of tossing and turning, he picks up his phone again.

This time, he scrolls through news articles, reads random stories, and dives into a rabbit hole of information. It's almost 3 a.m. before he finally drifts off.

Chapter Five

The Second Yoga Class

The alarm buzzes, pulling him from a restless sleep. His eyes are heavy, and his body feels sluggish, but he's committed to his new challenge. After a quick shower and a light breakfast, he heads back to the yoga studio.

The studio feels as serene as before. It feels like a lovely, welcoming place—like coming home. But this time, he's more aware of the contrast between its calm energy and his own restless mind. Grace welcomes the class and guides them into the first pose—a simple seated posture.

"Inhale deeply... exhale slowly," Grace instructs. "Feel the rhythm of your breath and let it guide your movements."

He tries to follow the instructions, slowing his breath to match her pace. It's improved a little but not much, and the deliberate slowness feels suffocating. His chest tightens, and it feels like he's choking himself.

"This is too slow. I can't do this," Harrison thinks to himself.

He manages for a little longer but then gives up. Instead, he shifts his focus to the postures, pushing deeper into each one. His hamstrings stretch further, his arms tremble slightly, but he powers through.

"The pain doesn't bother me. It's the breathing that's impossible," he tells himself.

Despite his struggle with the breath, the postures feel easier today. His arms don't feel as heavy, and his balance is improving. He notices small changes, his shoulders feel looser, his hips slightly more open.

When Grace guides the class into a challenging pose, he holds it longer than he expected. For a brief moment, he feels strong and present.

At the end of the class, Grace's voice is soft and soothing.

"Lie back. Let the body relax completely. Let go of all effort."

As he settles into Shavasana, his body melts into the mat. His breath slows naturally, and his mind goes quiet. It's a relief, like stepping out of a storm into stillness.

He doesn't remember falling asleep again, but when he opens his eyes, he feels refreshed. His body feels light, his mind calm.

As he rolls up his mat, he approaches the Grace.

"That was... easier today. I mean, physically. But the breathing—" He shakes his head. "It's still impossible for me."

She smiles gently. "It will come. You're learning to let go of control, to trust the rhythm of your body and breath. It takes time."

He understands this, but he has learned over the years that when you find a good teacher, investing in their time really speeds up your own development.

"I was wondering... do you do one-on-one sessions?" Harrison asks.

She tilts her head, studying him for a moment before nodding.

"I do. What's on your mind?"

He hesitates, rubbing the back of his neck. "I want to sit. Properly, I mean. Cross-legged, upright. I can't seem to manage it."

Her lips curl into a small smile. "That's a great goal. Let's schedule a session, and we'll work on it together."

The Following Day

The studio is quiet during the one-on-one, just the two of them on their mats in a softly lit corner. Grace sits cross-legged with ease, her posture perfectly upright, as Harrison mirrors her position—though with significantly more effort.

"So, you want to sit. Why is that so important to you?"

He pauses, thinking. "I met someone—a monk. He told me I couldn't still my mind until I could still my body. And he's right. My mind is... Chaotic. Sitting feels like the first step."

She nods, her expression thoughtful. "He is so right. Yoga is a complete science of which asanas are actually a small part. Yoga posses are called Asanas and were originally developed to still the body so you can sit and explore the deeper dimensions, but they have become an effective practice in themselves for stilling both the body and the mind."

"Let's start with your body. Your hips are tight, which is why sitting cross-legged feels so uncomfortable. We'll work on opening them up. But there's something else I noticed."

He raises an eyebrow, intrigued.

"Your breathing. It's all in your chest. You're in fight-or-flight mode constantly."

Her words hit him like a jolt. He's well aware of the concept, having studied it in relation to stress management and productivity. But hearing it applied to himself feels oddly personal.

"You're right," Harrison says. "I know about this stuff—I teach it to my clients. But I guess I've never thought about how I live in that state."

She nods gently. "Most of us do, especially when we're busy or stressed. Chest breathing excites the body—it's useful in the right context. But if you're always in that mode, it keeps your nervous system on high alert. To calm the body and mind, you need to breathe deeply into your belly."

The Breathing Lesson

She guides him into a reclined position, placing one hand lightly on her own abdomen.

"Place a hand on your belly. As you inhale, let your belly rise. Exhale slowly and let it fall."

He follows her lead, but his breath catches—his chest instinctively expands, his belly barely moving.

"It takes practice," Grace says. "Try emptying your lungs completely, then you should naturally use your belly when you inhale."

He tries again, focusing intently. This time, his belly rises slightly before his chest. It feels awkward, but there's a subtle shift—a moment of ease in his usually tight diaphragm.

"Breathing can be an incredibly powerful tool to control our mind," Grace explains. "When we're calm, we naturally breathe deeply. Slow, steady, through the belly. The breath reflects the state of the mind, and the mind reflects the breath. Learning to control your breath is learning to control your mind."

Harrison is really impressed—it's such a simple but effective tool that can be used to control your mind.

Targeted Stretches

Next, she introduces two specific stretches to open his hips:

Butterfly Pose: She guides him to sit with his feet together, knees falling outward. The stretch is intense, but she encourages him to relax into it rather than push, explaining there should be no sharp pain ever doing this.

Pigeon Pose: One leg bent in front, the other stretched behind. His hips ache, but he notices a sense of release as he holds the posture.

Throughout, she reminds him to breathe into his belly.

"The key is gentleness," Grace says. "Don't force it—let your body open naturally and use the relaxation of the exhale to further deepen the stretch."

At the end of the session, she gives him a short practice to do- three rounds of full yogic breath to energise him and clear the mind, followed by five minutes of triangle breathing to develop focus and concentration. He loves the practice and feels so good afterwards

QR code link to this practice: If you'd like to try this yourself.

SCAN ME

"Do this everyday," Grace advises. "It's short enough to fit into a busy schedule, but the consistency is what matters."

He nods, but deep down, he wonders how he'll find the time.

As the session winds down, she sits in the lotus position, looking at him thoughtfully.

"Balance is the key. Excitement and calm both have their place. But if you live only in excitement, you'll burn out. If you live only in calm, you'll stagnate. You can use your breath to be aware of how your body and mind is feeling, but also as a tool to bring balance to your life."

He nods slowly, the words sinking in.

"That makes sense. I guess I've been stuck in one mode-excited, driven all the time."

"That's common, especially for high achievers. But now you're learning to find balance."

As they work through the session, she explains the importance of the exhale.

"Exhaling is the body's way of releasing tension. It's natural, but we override it when we're stressed, distracted, or pushing too hard."

He furrows his brow. "So, half the time my body is naturally relaxing, but I don't let it because I'm not paying attention?"

She nods. "Exactly. Learning to focus on the exhale, to slow it down, helps us tap into that natural relaxation."

With his own practice and stretches, she recommends he comes to regular classes and joins in the community.

That evening, he sits at his desk, the room dimly lit by a single lamp. His journal lies open, the blank page waiting. He starts to write:

"Grace said I live in fight-or-flight mode. She's right. My breathing is often shallow and quick—it's the same when I'm drinking coffee, scrolling social media, or getting hyped about work. It keeps me wired, but it also keeps me tense."

"She said calm and excitement both have their place. I need to find the balance."

He pauses, tapping the pen against the page.

"I'm realising how much of my life excites me—coffee, social media even certain conversations. I need to be more mindful of when I'm feeding that energy. No wonder I am struggling to sleep, I am energising myself before bed, when I need to be calming down and slowing down."

"Exhaling is relaxing. Half the time my body wants to let go. Why don't I let it?"

He makes a decision- he needs to get some balance, so no more coffee after noon, no social media in the mornings or evenings. He writes it out clearly:

No work- emails, calls, social media or scrolling before 9 a.m. or after 6 p.m.

It feels like a monumental shift. But as he commits to it, he also feels a glimmer of hope.

Over the next few nights, the impact is immediate. Without coffee and social media late in the day, his sleep improves. It's still far from perfect, his mind races with thoughts of work and success, but it's better. He wakes up feeling more rested, and the mornings feel lighter without his usual phone scroll.

Still, the deeper struggle remains: his mind is caught in a loop, programmed for success and driven by a relentless need to achieve.

The week is a mix of highs and frustrations. Yoga classes are great, he really loves the community, it's a community of people seeking peace, it's a wonderful thing. His flexibility improves, and his body feels stronger and lighter. But fitting in the daily breathing practice is another story.

In the mornings, he's too busy and excited about work to sit still and make time. In the evenings, he's too tired. Days pass without him doing the practice, and guilt begins to creep in.

He writes in his journal “Why can't I find 10 minutes? I want to do this, but the day just slips away."

But he is really enjoying the yoga community. It's amazing having something like this so close to where he lives that can really start to bring balance to his life.

Chapter Six

A Breakthrough

Finally, after a week, he decides to dedicate time to the practice. He heads to the park, finding a quiet spot on the grass. Sitting comfortably, he closes his eyes and begins the breathing exercise.

At first, his mind is wandering, but full yogic breath is very engaging and after each round a sense of calm washes over him. He feels the sun on his face, hears the birds chirping, and notices his breath- slow, steady, grounding.

When he opens his eyes, he sees the monk sitting calmly in front of him, smiling warmly.

Harrison smiles back, feeling both surprised and deeply content.

"Congratulations. You can sit now. How do you feel?" the monk asks.

He thinks for a moment before answering.

"Better! My sleep is improving, my body feels great. But..." He hesitates. "My mind is still racing. I'm constantly thinking about work, success, my next goal. I can't seem to let it go."

"Well, I can see you have your own practice now, that's great. Your own practice is a very special thing. It can transform your life, if done consistently," the monk says.

Harrison shifts uncomfortably. "I am really struggling with the practice, I can't seem to fit it into my day."

The monk's eyes twinkle with humour.

"There are 1,440 minutes in a day, and you can't find 10 for yourself?"

Harrison laughs, realising the absurdity of it. The monk drops his serious look and smiles, his tone gentle but firm.

"A daily practice is powerful because it anchors you. It must take priority. Be the first thing you do each day. The mornings are easy to control, but evenings are full of distractions. Make it a habit first thing in your day: get up 15 minutes earlier."

Harrison nods, taking the advice to heart.

"Thank you so much for your help. I really feel I am starting to figure out how to balance my life again. In the last week, I've really noticed how much suffering there is. I really want to share this and help all the people. I could write a new book."

"You've done well. You have a lot of potential. But you must master this for yourself first before you teach," the monk says. "The West needs a fresh voice on happiness, and I can see you have that voice to share it. Will you come with me on a journey? I will teach you inner peace, and you can write a book to transform the suffering you see around you."

Harrison's breath catches. The invitation feels monumental. For an author, this is a dream, what an adventure.

"If you want to come, meet me here in one week. We will journey together to my monastery in the Himalayas. But remember—do your practice every day. It is the foundation of everything."

The monk rises, bowing slightly before walking away. Harrison sits for a long moment, the decision weighing on him, but his excitement growing.

Harrison returns home from the park, still feeling the warmth of the monk's words. He sits at his kitchen table, a mug of herbal tea in his hands—no coffee after noon now. The quiet of the evening settles around him, and he opens his journal to reflect.

He writes slowly, pausing between thoughts: "First, still the body. Then, still the mind. Yoga taught me that. I couldn't even sit until my body began to loosen.

I've also learned that certain things excite me—coffee, social media, even intense conversations. Those things have their place, but not before bed. Other things, like slowing down my breath or reading something calming, help me wind down.

Work too needs clear boundaries. A start and stop time. Without that, it spills into everything else, keeping my mind racing even when the day is over.

And then there's consistency. The monk made me see how hard it is to commit to just 10 minutes a day. But that's the point. It's not about intensity—it's about showing up."

He underlines the last sentence twice.

Closing the journal, he picks up his laptop and searches: "Who has daily routines?" The results fascinate him—stories of great thinkers, athletes, and successful entrepreneurs all emphasising the importance of consistency.

Benjamin Franklin: "Morning routines for clarity." Serena Williams: "Daily practice for excellence." Steve Jobs: “Consistent habits for focus.”

"They all had routines," Harrison thinks to himself. "It's not just about discipline—it's about creating a foundation."

He bookmarks a few articles to read later but resolves to focus on his own practice first.

The Week of Consistency

The next morning, he wakes 15 minutes earlier than usual. It feels strange, like borrowing time from himself, but he sits on the mat, remembering the monk's advice. He begins the breathing practice. At first, his mind wanders, tugged by to-do lists and fleeting thoughts. But the full breaths are so engaging, it's like they scrub his mind clear. After this, his breath steadies, his body relaxes, and his mind grows clear.

After 10 minutes, he opens his eyes, feeling refreshed. He writes in his journal: "It's like I cleaned my mind. Starting the day like this feels... powerful."

Midweek: Building Strength

By the third day, practising first thing feels completely natural. His body settles more easily into the rhythm, and his mind resists less. He notices the difference throughout his day:

- Fewer distractions at work
- A calmer response to challenges
- Greater focus and energy

He writes: "The morning practice isn't just a routine—it's a foundation. It sets the tone for the day. I feel stronger, clearer, and more grounded."

End of the Week: A Breakthrough

On the penultimate morning, he sits for his practice with a sense of anticipation. The breathing feels natural now and his body relaxes almost immediately. By the end, his mind feels light, like the lingering tension has been swept away.

He opens his journal and reflects upon the week: "I don't have to fear diving fully into work or life. No matter what happens during the day, I know I can clear my mind each morning. This practice is my anchor."

Throughout the week, he notices how this daily consistency builds strength:

- His productivity soars because his mind is uncluttered
- He enjoys his evenings more because work doesn't bleed into them
- His sleep continues to improve, with fewer restless nights

The routine has already become a non-negotiable part of his day, something he looks forward to rather than dreads. By the end of the week, he feels a newfound confidence.

Reflection and Progress

That evening, he writes in his journal: "Consistency is the key. It's not about doing something big all at once—it's about showing up every day, even for just 15 minutes. This week, I've built a foundation I can rely on."

"The monk was right. A daily practice isn't a chore—it's a gift. It clears my mind, calms my body, and gives me strength."

"Next week, the journey continues. I feel ready."

On the final morning, he wakes early, fully energised and excited about the adventure ahead. He decides to start early in the park with his daily practice.

The park is quiet in the early morning, the sun casting long shadows across the grass. Harrison arrives with his large rucksack slung over one shoulder, packed as lightly as he could manage. He's travelled before, but this feels different. This isn't a holiday or a business trip—this is something deeper, a true adventure.

The monk is waiting for him on a bench near the tree where they first met. His simple robe is loose around his frame, and his serene smile greets him like a warm embrace.

"Ah, you're here. Ready for the journey?" the monk asks.

Harrison nods, shifting the weight of his bag.

"I've tried to pack light, but it wasn't easy. I'm not sure what I'll need."

The monk chuckles softly.

"That's a good start—packing light. You'll learn you always have everything you need. For now, sit. Let us settle for a few minutes before we begin."

The monk gestures to the grass, and they sit cross-legged beneath the shade of the tree.

Harrison adjusts his position, the ground slightly uneven beneath him. The monk closes his eyes, his posture effortlessly straight, his hands resting lightly on his knees. For a moment, Harrison feels his familiar excited energy—anticipation for the journey ahead, a mix of nervousness and eagerness.

But then he remembers his practice. He lets his shoulders drop, focuses on his breath, and begins to settle. As he goes through his practice the excitement softens, and he notices the warmth of the sun on his face, the sound of birds, the gentle rustle of leaves. His body feels at ease, his mind quieter than it has been in years.

The Monk Speaks: A Lesson on Desires

After several minutes of silence, the monk opens his eyes, his gaze calm and steady.

"As I promised, let us start by talking about desires."

Harrison leans forward slightly, intrigued.

"Every action we perform is to fulfil a desire. Say you're lying in bed. Why do you open your eyes?"

Harrison considers this for a moment. "Because I want to see?"

The monk nods. "Exactly. Why do you put your feet on the floor?"

"Because I want to stand."

"Yes. Every action is driven by a desire. Now, every desire exists because we want to feel good."

Harrison tilts his head, curious.

"Say you desire a coffee. Why?"

"Because it'll make me feel good."

"Exactly. Say you desire money. Why?"

"So I can buy things... that will make me feel good."

The monk smiles, letting this sink in for a moment.

"Every desire, big or small, is because we want to feel good. Now, let me ask you—what is your biggest desire? Your life's ambition?"

Harrison doesn't need to think long. He's held this vision for years.

"To retire on an island with my family. To have enough money to take care of everyone, so no one has to work again. We'd all just relax and enjoy our time together in paradise."

The monk nods, as though he expected this answer.

"And how will you feel when you achieve this?"

Harrison's voice softens as he answers.

"I'll feel relaxed. The race will be over. No more need to strive, no more pushing. Everyone I love will be safe and secure. It'll be peaceful."

The monk smiles deeply, his voice kind.

"So your biggest desire is to be at peace. To truly feel at peace."

The words settle over Harrison like a wave. The monk continues.

"In fact, everyone's biggest desire is this. Every single desire—coffee, money, success, even your island dream—is because we want to feel at peace. We want to know that we are okay."

Harrison nods slowly, the truth sinking in.

"Here's the good news- your default nature is okay. Peace is your natural state. But we forget this because we chase desires, thinking they will bring us peace, when peace is already within us."

Harrison looks down, processing the monk's words. His life has been one long chase—striving, achieving, reaching for something that would make him feel complete. But the idea that peace is already within him feels both comforting and challenging.

"If peace is my default, why am I always chasing it?" Harrison asks.

The monk watches him with a knowing smile, giving him space to reflect.

"That is a question you must learn to answer for yourself," the monk replies.

The monk stands, dusting off his robe, and gestures toward the path ahead.

"Come. Let's walk. There's much to see, and much to learn. This journey is about discovering the peace that's already within you. And it begins now."

Harrison rises, adjusting his rucksack. His steps feel lighter, his breath slower. As they walk, he feels a small but growing sense of clarity.

For the first time in years, he isn't chasing. He's simply moving forward, trusting the path.

London slowly comes to life as Harrison and the monk leave Hyde Park, the monk's pace unhurried despite the bustling city around them. He adjusts the straps of his rucksack, his mind already whirring with questions about their journey.

"So, how are we getting to your monastery? A flight to India or Nepal?"

The monk smiles but doesn't answer directly.

"You must learn to focus on the present. If you're always looking forward, you will miss the joy found in the constant surprises that the present brings. So let's start with today—we start with the train."

Harrison smiles, realising he was striving again, and feels a deep sense of gratitude to have this amazing monk in his life.

Chapter Seven

The Underground Experience

As they descend into the tube station, Harrison feels the familiar crush of London's morning commute. The air is thick with the scent of damp coats and hurried bodies. The crowd presses in on them as they move towards the platform.

The monk moves slowly, seemingly unaffected by the rush. His steps are deliberate, his gaze soft, as though he's taking in the experience as a curious observer. Despite the packed space, he rarely bumps into anyone, flowing effortlessly through the crowd.

Harrison, on the other hand, struggles to remain calm. People jostle past, brushing against his rucksack, and the hum of conversation grates on his nerves. He glances at the monk, amazed by his serene expression.

"How is he not irritated by this chaos?" Harrison thinks to himself.

When the train arrives, the doors slide open with a hiss, and people surge forward. Harrison winces as someone elbows past him to get inside. The monk waits patiently, stepping aboard with a calm fluidity. Inside, there are no seats, so they stand near the door, gripping the poles as the train lurches forward.

Harrison's frustration builds as more passengers crowd in, their bags pressing against him. A tall man in a suit leans into the monk, who simply steps aside slightly, smiling faintly as though amused.

Finally, Harrison can't contain his irritation.

"Doesn't it bother you? The pushing, the rudeness?"

The monk turns to him, his voice gentle. "There is no rudeness."

Harrison blinks, incredulous. "What do you mean? That guy just shoved past us without even saying sorry!"

The monk's expression remains calm as the train sways.

"There is no rudeness, only your rules. Your rules say that when someone brushes past you, they must apologise. His rules say that getting on the train quickly is more important."

Harrison frowns, considering this.

"Your rules make him rude. His rules make him not rude. All people believe they are good. All people are striving for one thing: to feel good. Perhaps his rushing makes him feel good because he thinks it will save him time."

Harrison leans back against the door, processing this.

"So you're saying... everyone has different rules? And we just make them up?"

The monk nods. "Exactly. No two people have the same rules. But when you let go of your rules, you free yourself from the suffering they create."

Harrison glances around the crowded train. A woman shuffles closer, her bag bumping his side, and he starts to bristle but stops himself. "My rules," he thinks, trying to let go of the expectation that she should move aside or apologise.

For a brief moment, he feels lighter. The irritation doesn't vanish completely, but it fades, leaving room for curiosity.

"Maybe she's just tired. Or distracted. Maybe she's not even aware of her bag," he thinks to himself.

The monk catches his gaze and smiles, as though sensing the shift.

"Likes and dislikes shape our experience of life. You disliked the train, so it brought you frustration. But if you let go of your dislike, the train simply becomes what it is- a train. Nothing more, nothing less."

The train sways as it barrels through the underground tunnels. Harrison shifts his weight against the pole, looking at the monk with a mix of frustration and curiosity.

"I get what you're saying about rules, but... politeness isn't just made up. It's cultural. It's common. Everyone knows it's rude to push past someone without saying sorry."

The monk turns to him, his gaze steady and calm.

"You must start to see reality with clarity. Don't believe what I say—investigate it for yourself. By internal inspection, test what is real. If it's real, keep it. If it's not real, reject it."

Harrison frowns, intrigued but unconvinced.

"Okay, but politeness is real. It's not just me. It's cultural—something we all share."

The monk's expression softens, his voice patient.

"Where did you learn your rules about politeness? Did you find an exact guide, a universal book that everyone reads?"

Harrison opens his mouth to respond but stops. The monk continues.

"Your rules come from many sources. Your parents, your teachers, your friends. From TV shows, books, social media, even strangers you've observed. They are a patchwork of influences unique to your life."

He gestures subtly to the crowded train.

"No two people have the same rules. And yet we walk around expecting others to behave according to our made-up set of rules. When they don't, we suffer."

Harrison looks at the people around them—the man with the briefcase who had pushed past earlier, a woman scrolling through her phone, a teenager with headphones nodding to music. He realises the monk is right: their lives, their experiences, their rules are all different.

"But politeness—how people treat each other—surely there's something universal about that?"

The monk shakes his head gently.

"Cultures have patterns, yes. But within a culture, do all people behave the same way? Even among your family, your closest friends, are their rules for politeness exactly the same as yours?"

Harrison hesitates.

"Well, no, not exactly. But there are common ideas, right?"

The monk nods thoughtfully.

"Common ideas, perhaps. But no absolutes. For every person who shares your idea of politeness, there is another who does not. Why would you want to rule out liking so many people in the world because of your made-up rules?"

Harrison's frustration begins to shift into curiosity. He looks out the window as the dark tunnel flashes by, reflecting on what the monk said.

"So my rules... they're just made up? Pieces of everything I've experienced. They're not real, just rules I picked up along the way," he thinks to himself.

He thinks about the times he's felt anger or disappointment when someone didn't behave as he expected:

- A friend arriving late
- A client cancelling a meeting
- A stranger cutting in line

"All those times I got upset... it wasn't because of what they did. It was because of my rules."

The train slows as they approach the next station. The monk looks at Harrison with a kind smile.

"The question is not whether your rules are good or bad. The question is whether they help you or harm you. Do they bring you peace? Or do they create suffering?"

Harrison exhales slowly, realising the weight of the question. He thinks of how often his rules have created stress, anger, or disappointment.

"This is why internal inspection is so important. Don't hold on to a rule just because it feels familiar. Investigate. If it causes suffering, let it go."

The train stops, and the doors slide open. People push past again, but this time Harrison doesn't feel the same surge of irritation. He watches the faces of the commuters—a mixture of weariness, focus, and urgency. He imagines their rules: the parent rushing to pick up their child, the worker desperate not to miss their train.

For the first time, he feels something shift inside him. The anger isn't gone completely, but it's quieter—softened by a growing awareness of how his own mind shapes his experience.

The central station buzzes with life—travellers rushing past, the hum of announcements, and the clatter of suitcases on tile. The monk and Harrison find a quiet corner, setting their bags down. Harrison pulls out his notebook and pen, leaning on a wall.

"I need to write this down. If I don't, I'll forget it."

The monk nods, his gaze wandering over the passing crowds.

"Writing is good. It solidifies what you've learned."

Harrison smiles faintly.

"It's always been my superpower—taking what I've learned and making it stick. It's how I've been able to succeed."

Writing About Rules

Harrison bends over his notebook, pen scratching against the page. He writes:

"Rules are made up. They come from everywhere—parents, friends, teachers, books, strangers—but no two people have the same ones."

"My rules create suffering when I expect others to follow them. Like on the train, when people bumped into me and didn't apologise, it wasn't rudeness—it was my expectation clashing with their rules."

"Let go of rules that don't serve you. Investigate them. If they cause pain, let them go."

He underlines the last sentence, then leans back, satisfied.

"This is something I need to practise," he thinks to himself. "I'm already seeing how much better life can be without clinging to my rules."

Chapter Eight

The Coffee Experience

Harrison closes his notebook and stretches. "I haven't had a coffee today. Do you want one?"

The monk shakes his head. "I'm fine, thank you."

"Are you not thirsty?"

The monk pats a small water bottle tucked into his bag. "I have water."

Harrison makes his way to the coffee shop. The line is long, but he's feeling calm, buoyed by his reflections. When it's his turn, he orders confidently.

"A large Americano with hot milk on the side, please."

He steps aside to watch the barista, practising what the monk taught him about rules. He notices how busy the café is. The barista juggling orders with quick, precise movements. But then he sees her pour cold milk directly into his coffee.

His stomach tightens, frustration bubbling up. "That's not what I asked for." But he catches himself, trying to shift his perspective.

"She's busy. The system probably got the order wrong. It's no one's fault," he thinks to himself.

He takes the coffee and a bottle of water for the monk. The cup feels cool in his hand—a sign that the coffee isn't as hot as he likes. He sighs but decides to let it go.

The cold coffee and sparkling Water

Back at their spot, he hands the monk the water and sits down. The monk unscrews the cap, and a hiss escapes as bubbles rise to the surface.

Harrison's eyes widen. "Oh no. They gave you sparkling water instead of still. I'm sorry—they got both our orders wrong."

The monk takes a sip, his smile widening. "It's lovely, actually. What a change. I rarely drink sparkling water."

Harrison stares, incredulous. "But it's not what you wanted. My coffee's cold, your water's wrong... This is so frustrating."

The monk chuckles softly. "Ah, this is a good lesson. Your likes and dislikes are strong with coffee."

"Likes Don't Benefit You"

Harrison furrows his brow. "How can likes not benefit me? Surely liking something is good?"

The monk sets the bottle down, his gaze thoughtful.

"When you like something very specifically, you exclude so many other possibilities. You like your coffee one way, so there are thousands of other coffees you can no longer enjoy."

He gestures to Harrison's cup.

"You also stop truly experiencing that thing. When your coffee matches your expectations, you switch off—you don't taste it fully, savour it, or enjoy its uniqueness. Every coffee is unique. How can you taste that if you are under the illusion that you want it the same every time?"

Harrison takes a sip of his coffee. It's lukewarm, and the milk is wrong, but he tries to focus on the flavour rather than his expectations.

"Okay, dislikes are easier to understand. Everything I dislike becomes something I suffer, like rudeness or busy trains."

The monk nods. "Exactly. Imagine how small you make your life every time you decide to dislike something. You cut off entire experiences, entire possibilities, just because they don't match your preferences."

The monk takes on a more serious tone.

"Dislikes are especially harmful with people. When you dislike someone, you must keep remembering why you dislike them—otherwise, you'll forget. So you repeat the reasons over and over in your mind. This creates suffering for you, not them."

Harrison's eyes widen as he thinks about the people in his life he's struggled to get along with. He realises how often he's replayed their faults in his mind, reinforcing his own frustration.

"Imagine how many people in your life you do this with," the monk continues. "Just one is enough to cause you pain. Multiply that, and you shrink your world even further."

Harrison sits back, holding his coffee. It's not hot, and it's not perfect, but as he takes another sip, he tries to taste it fully—the bitterness, the slight sweetness, the unique flavour.

"Every coffee is unique. Every moment is unique. Why do I keep trying to make them all the same?" he thinks to himself.

The monk watches him with a faint smile. "You're beginning to see. Likes and dislikes narrow your experience of life. But when you loosen their grip, you can experience things as they truly are."

Harrison takes another sip of his lukewarm coffee, glancing at the monk, who is quietly sipping his sparkling water with a serene expression. He looks at the cup in his hand, the frustration still lingering at the edges of his mind, but then something shifts.

"This isn't just any coffee," he thinks to himself. "This is my first coffee on this adventure. My first coffee with this amazing monk."

The thought settles over him, softening his frustration. He sips again, this time paying attention to the flavour—the slight bitterness, the earthy warmth. It's different from what he expected, but there's something unique about it.

He lets his gaze wander to the bustling café, his thoughts drifting to the girl who made the coffee. She looked tired, her movements hurried but precise, doing her best in the chaos of the busy shop.

"She really tried. She probably didn't even realise the milk was cold. How kind of her to still do her best, even when she looks so worn out."

He smiles faintly, a feeling of gratitude blooming in his chest. He glances at the monk, who seems completely at ease, and decides to mirror him. He slows his breathing, relaxes his grip on the cup, and takes another sip, savouring the moment.

As he drinks, the familiar caffeine buzz begins to set in—a light, pleasant energy spreading through his body. He notices it without judgement, enjoying the sensation for what it is.

"Even this—this little kick of energy is something to appreciate. It's not just about the taste. It's about the whole experience," he thinks.

He glances at his watch. They still have 20 minutes until the train. Normally, he'd be checking his phone, rushing through his drink, fidgeting with impatience. But now, he leans back slightly, letting the atmosphere of the station wash over him.

The hum of voices, the clatter of luggage, the warmth of the coffee in his hand—it all feels richer, more vivid.

"This slowness... it's nice. It's not something I usually allow myself, but it feels good to just sit and enjoy."

He smiles, taking another sip, and for the first time, he feels fully present.

The monk glances at him, his gaze warm and knowing. "How is the coffee?"

Harrison grins. "It's... special. Not what I expected, but better in a way."

The monk nods approvingly. "You're learning."

They sit in companionable silence, the monk sipping his sparkling water, Harrison savouring his coffee. For those few moments, the world seems to slow down, and Harrison feels something he hasn't felt in years: contentment.

As the train pulls into the platform, Harrison watches the crowd begin to surge forward. Normally, he'd feel a twinge of irritation at the jostling and pushing, but today, he breathes deeply and reminds himself: "These are my made-up rules. They don't have to control me."

He moves with the crowd, his steps slow and deliberate. When someone brushes past him, he doesn't react—just observes the moment. He notices how freeing it feels to let go of the tension he'd normally carry.

"I'm in control of my experience. It's not perfect, but it's stable. Steady," he thinks to himself.

Once on the train, Harrison turns to the monk. "Where do you want to sit?"

The monk scans the cabin, his gaze settling on a set of four seats facing each other, two of them already occupied by a young couple. He gestures toward the aisle seat, leaving the window seat for Harrison.

Harrison's instinct is to ask for the window seat facing a other way, but he catches himself.

"That's just a preference. I don't need it to enjoy the journey," he thinks to himself.

He takes the seat instead, settling in beside the monk. To his surprise, he feels perfectly fine, even a quiet sense of accomplishment.

Chapter Nine

The Lesson on Expectations

As the train begins to move, Harrison leans forward, speaking softly so as not to disturb the couple across from them.

"I'm noticing something. Normally, I'd feel frustrated about not getting the seat I wanted, or about the crowd pushing to get on. But letting go of those preferences—it's like I'm in control of my experience. It's much more... steady. Even enjoyable."

The monk smiles warmly, nodding. "Well done. You are picking this up quickly. Our likes, dislikes, and rules are all expectations—how we expect things to be."

The monk's tone becomes thoughtful, his voice low and calm.

"Expectations have benefits. We have evolved to have them because they reduce the need for constant decision-making. Think about it: you expect a chair to take your weight, so you sit without checking it. This saves time."

Harrison nods, intrigued.

"You expect your car to be safe, the steering wheel to steer, the brakes to stop the car. Without these expectations, you'd need to inspect every detail before each journey, like a pilot inspecting a plane. This efficiency has allowed us to do more, to create complex systems, and to evolve into the dominant species on the planet."

The monk pauses, looking out the window as the train speeds past cityscapes.

"But expectations have a significant negative effect on our enjoyment of life."

Harrison tilts his head. "How so?"

"Because you expect the sun to rise each morning, you no longer truly experience it as the miraculous event it is. You expect your phone to send messages and make calls, but you've lost the wonder at this incredible feat of engineering."

Harrison sits back, reflecting. The monk continues.

"Your friends, your family—you expect your mother to be excited to hear from you, to help you, to be loving. So you no longer fully appreciate it. Every time you expect something, you stop truly experiencing it."

The monk leans forward slightly, his voice softer but full of conviction.

"Imagine if you had no expectations. Everything in life would become a wonderful surprise. A gift. You'd see things for what they truly are, without the lens of how you think they should be."

Harrison's mind races as he processes the idea. He thinks about his own expectations—how often he assumes things will be a certain way:

- The perfect coffee

- A seamless workday
- His friends and family always behaving as he hopes

"How many of those moments have I missed because I was too focused on what they weren't?" he thinks to himself.

As the monk finishes speaking, Harrison gazes out the window. The sun is breaking through the clouds, casting a golden light over the passing fields. For the first time, he notices the way the light dances on the glass, the intricate patterns of shadow and movement.

He takes a deep breath, savouring the moment.

"I've seen a sunrise thousands of times, but I've never really seen it. Not like this," he thinks to himself.

He looks back at the monk, who is watching him with a gentle smile.

"I see what you mean. Expectations... they make life smaller. Duller."

The monk nods. "And when you let go of them, life expands. It becomes vivid, alive."

Harrison smiles faintly, glancing at the couple across from them, the movement of the train, the soft hum of conversation in the background. For the first time, he feels like he's not just moving through the world—he's part of it.

Writing in the Notebook

The train hums softly as it speeds through the countryside, the gentle sway lulling the passengers into a quiet calm. Harrison pulls out his notebook again, flipping to a fresh page. The monk watches him with quiet approval as Harrison begins to write.

He captures his thoughts carefully:

"Likes and dislikes narrow our world. Every time I decide I like something in a very specific way, I close myself off from experiencing it any other way. And with dislikes, I create my own suffering by rejecting so much of life."

"Expectations save time and reduce decision-making, but they also blind us to the beauty of the present moment. When we expect the sun to rise, we stop marvelling at it. When we expect kindness from a friend, we stop appreciating it for the gift it is."

"Letting go of expectations allows us to see life as it truly is—a series of unique, surprising, and wondrous moments."

He underlines the last sentence, sitting back with a faint smile.

The monk shifts slightly in his seat, settling into the rhythm of the journey. Harrison glances at him, hesitant.

"Letting go of expectations, likes, and dislikes—it feels so hard. I get what you're saying, and I'm trying, but sometimes it feels like I'm fighting myself. How do I keep going without feeling frustrated or discouraged?"

The monk nods, his expression kind. "It is hard. It's also not something you should try to achieve all at once."

The monk breathes gently, his tone calm and measured.

"You must take it gently, step by step. This understanding will grow with time and practice. Frustration comes from wanting to change too quickly, from expecting yourself to already be at the end of the journey. Don't aim to be perfect. Perfection itself can become a strong desire, leaving you unhappy until it is fulfilled."

Harrison frowns, thinking. This is his default—to strive, to try and be perfect.

"Instead, we are gently increasing your awareness of reality, expanding your conscious control of your experience. Some of this comes through knowledge and understanding, like the lessons we've discussed. The rest comes through practice—applying what you've learned, observing your mind, and adjusting as you go."

Harrison exhales, the monk's words settling over him like a warm blanket. He thinks of how far he's already come—his ability to sit, the small victories in letting go of preferences, and the moments of clarity he's experienced.

"So, it's not about being perfect. It's about making progress."

The monk smiles, a flicker of pride in his eyes. "Exactly. Awareness grows gently, like a flame catching on dry wood. Tend to it patiently, and it will illuminate your life."

Harrison nods slowly, taking in the monk's words.

"But there's something even more important than progress," the monk adds.

Harrison tilts his head, curious.

"Treat yourself with the same kindness and care you would give to someone else. Be gentle with yourself. You're learning something new—an entirely new way of experiencing life. Of course, it will take time. Of course, you will stumble."

The monk pauses, his voice becoming softer.

"Start with yourself. Bring gentleness into your life. Speak to yourself as you would a dear friend. When you falter, forgive yourself. When you struggle, encourage yourself. Kindness begins with you."

Harrison nods, a sense of calm washing over him. He turns back to his notebook, writing down the monk's words to ensure he won't forget them.

He sits back, the monk's words settling into him. He realises how often he's been harsh with himself—pushing to succeed, judging his mistakes, expecting perfection. He looks at the notebook in his lap, the neatly written notes a testament to his drive to improve.

"I've always been kind to others. Why is it so hard to be kind to myself?" he thinks.

He picks up the pen and writes: "Be gentle. Be kind. Speak to yourself like a friend."

He underlines the sentence, feeling a small but profound shift inside him.

As the train rolls on, Harrison writes one final note: "This journey isn't about perfection. It's about progress. Each step brings me closer to understanding and controlling my experience. Letting go of likes, dislikes, and expectations isn't easy, but it's freeing. For the first time, I feel like I'm beginning to see life as it truly is."

He closes the notebook and leans back in his seat, watching the countryside blur past the window.

The monk watches him with a faint smile.

"The path is not just about letting go of expectations for others. It's also about letting go of expectations for yourself. Progress comes not from force, but from patience and care. Treat yourself gently, and the journey will unfold naturally."

Harrison nods, a quiet determination growing within him. He closes his notebook, gazing out the window at the passing scenery. The sunlight flickers through the trees, casting a warm glow over the cabin.

For the first time, he feels a sense of ease—not because he's mastered the teachings, but because he's beginning to understand that mastery isn't the goal. The journey is about kindness, patience, and steady growth, one gentle step at a time.

The train glides steadily along the tracks, the rhythm of its movement a soothing backdrop. Harrison sits quietly, his notebook again open on his lap. The monk is resting, his eyes closed and his breathing deep and even. Taking advantage of the quiet, Harrison flips back through his notes, rereading what he's written over the past few days.

He pulls out his pen and begins to write again, summarising what he's learned so far:

Lesson One: Stillness "First, still the body, then the mind. Yoga taught me that. I couldn't even sit until my body began to loosen and relax. Stillness starts with the physical—it's the foundation for everything else."

Lesson Two: Balance "I've learned how much my daily habits affect my experience of life. Some things excite me, like coffee, social media, and success-driven conversations. Other things calm me, like breathing practices, yoga, and clear boundaries for work. Balance comes from understanding these effects and creating a structure that supports both calm and productivity."

Lesson Three: Consistency "A daily practice is key. I know how hard it is to fit just 15 minutes into my day, but doing it every morning has been transformative. It clears my mind and anchors me. Consistency is where real progress happens—not perfection, just showing up every day."

Lesson Four: Desires "All my desires are to feel good, to know that I am OK. I must understand: my default setting is OK. I am always OK. It is only when I desire something that I lose sight of this. I desire something because I believe I am not OK until I get that thing. So, when I desire something, I must just know that I am OK, feel that, and let myself feel good and safe."

Lesson Five: Rules "Rules are made up. They're unique to each of us, shaped by our experiences, but they often create suffering for us when we expect others to follow them. Letting go of my rules has already made me calmer and more open to life as it is, not as I think it should be."

Lesson Six: Likes and Dislikes "Likes and dislikes narrow my world. When I cling to a specific preference, I close myself off to other possibilities. Dislikes are even worse—they shrink my life and create suffering. By loosening the grip of likes and dislikes, I can experience things as they truly are."

Lesson Seven: Expectations "Expectations save time and make life more efficient, but they also rob us of wonder. When I expect something to be a certain way, I stop appreciating it for what it is.

Letting go of expectations helps me see the world with fresh eyes, as if everything is a gift or a surprise."

Lesson Eight: Gentleness "Treat yourself with kindness and care. Be gentle with yourself, as you would with a dear friend. This journey isn't about being perfect—it's about making progress, one small step at a time. Gentleness is what makes that possible."

Harrison pauses, reading back over his summary. A small smile spreads across his face as he realises how much he's already learned. For years, he'd been stuck in a cycle of striving and dissatisfaction, always chasing the next thing. Now, for the first time, he feels like he's stepping off that treadmill and into something more meaningful.

"I'm not there yet, but I'm moving in the right direction. That's enough for now," he thinks to himself.

He writes one final thought at the bottom of the page: "This journey isn't just about learning—it's about unlearning. Letting go of old habits, old patterns, and seeing life as it truly is. One step at a time."

He closes the notebook and leans back, watching the countryside roll by. The monk opens his eyes, glancing at him with a knowing smile.

"You look at peace," the monk says.

Harrison grins. "For now, I am. Thanks to you."

The monk chuckles softly. "A teacher learns much from teaching"

Chapter Ten

A Deeper Way to Relax

The buzz of the airport surrounds them—snippets of announcements, the clatter of luggage, and the hum of travellers moving through the terminal. The monk walks calmly, his steps deliberate as Harrison scans the departure board.

"Our flight's to Mumbai, right?"

The monk nods, his hands loosely clasped behind his back.

"It's in four hours. That gives us plenty of time to relax. How about we find a bar? I could use a drink."

The monk smiles faintly as they walk toward a quieter corner of the terminal. "I don't drink alcohol."

Harrison raises an eyebrow, intrigued. "Really, never? Why not?"

The monk's expression remains gentle, but there's a spark of curiosity in his eyes. "Because alcohol dampens my experience of life. I prefer to feel good without external stimulants."

Harrison stops, turning to face him fully. "How can that be? A drink makes me feel amazing—it relaxes me, helps me switch off, forget about work, success, and all that stress. It makes me have fun more easily."

The monk nods thoughtfully. "I see. That is a nice thing. But let me show you something: how to feel that way without needing a drink."

"Really? That would be amazing."

The monk gestures to a nearby seating area, and they settle into chairs by a large window overlooking the runway.

"To understand this, you must first grasp a key idea: our whole experience is internal."

Harrison leans forward, sceptical. "Internal? What do you mean? Isn't it external—we experience what's happening around us?"

The monk chuckles softly. "Most people believe that. This leads them to believe external things bring them pleasure. However, we create our whole experience internally. We are completely in charge of our experience, and with practice, you can choose how to respond to every moment of your life."

"But let's break it down. Start with your eyes. When you see an object, how do you see it?"

Harrison pauses, considering. "I guess... light bounces off the object and into my eyes?"

The monk nods. "Exactly. Your eyes absorb this light, translate it into an electrical signal, and send this up the optic nerve to the brain. The brain processes this signal, recognises the object, and only then do you experience it. Your experience isn't of the object itself, but of the interpretation your brain creates."

Harrison's eyes widen.

"So an external object, let's say you see a pretty face—this is external. Your experience is not of the object, not of the light reflected off the object, not of the signal up the optic nerve. Your experience is internal after the brain has processed the signal. Your brain recognises a face, it then recognises it to match your criteria as a pretty face, and you choose to feel good."

"Wow," Harrison says. "So say I see a car I like, I see an external object, my brain says it's a nice car and I feel good inside. Or if it's a bad car, I feel bad inside."

"Exactly."

"So the object doesn't make me feel good. It's my likes and dislikes that make me feel good or bad internally."

"The same applies to all your senses," the monk continues. "Let us take hearing. Someone says you look good in a suit. Your eardrum picks up the vibration of their voice, translates this into an electric signal which travels up a nerve to the brain, your brain processes the statement, and at this point after the brain, you feel good."

"What about touch? That doesn't feel external?"

"You're right, it feels much more internal. But it's still external. Let's say you touch something slimy with your hand—your fingers send an electrical signal to the brain, the brain interprets this signal as slimy, and only after this do you experience the object internally and feel bad or good if you like slimy. The same is true for taste and smell. Your whole experience is internal. Now you know this, it can really grow into your ability to control your experience to feel good at will, but this is something that grows with practice."

"Wow, this is incredible," Harrison says. "It's so simple and obvious but a complete revelation."

"Let's try something. Close your eyes."

Harrison closes his eyes.

"I want you to really tap into how you feel when you have a drink of alcohol. Imagine taking that first satisfying sip, now feel the relief, the relaxation, the satisfaction. Let this flow through your body. Can you feel all the past experiences of this sensation? Tap into them, let them flow."

Harrison sits silently, his face softening as he immerses himself in the exercise. After a few minutes, the monk speaks again.

"When you're ready, gently open your eyes. How do you feel?"

Harrison opens his eyes, blinking slowly. "I feel... really relaxed. Like I've actually had a drink."

The monk smiles. "You see? You don't need an external stimulant to feel good. With practice, you can create these feelings within yourself, anytime you choose."

Harrison shakes his head, amazed.

Harrison leaned back, still savouring the relaxed state the monk had guided him into. The monk stretched slightly and gestured toward an open space near the edge of the terminal.

"Next, we'll do some yoga to release tension from the body and mind. A long flight can make the body stiff, so it's wise to prepare with ease and relaxation."

Harrison hesitated, glancing around. "Yoga? Here? Where will we have space?"

The monk chuckled softly. "We only need two metres each."

"But it's so busy. Won't it be distracting with all the sounds and people?"

The monk's smile deepened. "This is a common misunderstanding. People assume you need total silence and serenity to practise. But practising in a busy place is an excellent exercise. It allows you to break free from many incorrect beliefs. Let the external sounds go—they're not part of your practice."

They found a quiet corner, rolling out their mats. To his surprise, no one seemed to mind. A few passers-by even paused to watch with smiles of curiosity or approval.

As they sat cross-legged to begin, he noticed how natural it suddenly felt.

"I was worried about how strange this would look, but no one cares," he thought to himself. "It's just me and the monk here, practising."

The monk guided him through a series of gentle postures, focusing on slow, deliberate movements. With each stretch, he felt his body loosening, the tension of the day melting away.

"Lengthen your breath as you move," the monk instructed. "Feel the inhale stretch your body, and the exhale release all tension."

Harrison followed, his breath deepening. At first, the hum of the terminal distracted him, but as he focused on the postures, the sounds faded into the background. With every movement, his body opened up, and his mind grew quieter.

The practice ended with shavasana. He lay flat on his back, arms at his sides, palms facing upward.

"Let go completely," the monk said softly. "Feel the ground supporting you. The work is done. Now, just be."

As he lay there, he felt a profound sense of peace. His breath was slow and steady, his body light and relaxed. The sounds of the airport seemed distant, almost soothing.

When he opened his eyes, he felt refreshed, as if he'd woken from a deep sleep. He sat up slowly, glancing at the monk, who smiled at him warmly.

"That was amazing. I feel completely at peace. Much more relaxed than from a few drinks."

"Yoga is not just about the body. It's a way to align the body, breath, and mind. Now, you're ready for the journey ahead."

Harrison nodded, a quiet smile spreading across his face. For the first time in years, he felt truly content and ready—not just for the flight, but for whatever lay ahead.

After their yoga practice, they spent the remaining time before their flight relaxing. They sat quietly, enjoying the rhythm of the airport. The monk seemed perfectly at ease, and Harrison found himself mirroring that calm.

For a while, there was no rush—just the peaceful sense of being present. But as the time to board approached, the mood in the terminal shifted, and Harrison's sense of ease began to waver.

As they joined the boarding line, he initially felt fine. He stood patiently, observing the people around him, focusing on his breath. But ten minutes in, his patience began to fray. The line moved slowly, and his thoughts started to wander.

"Why aren't they moving faster? This is ridiculous," he thought to himself.

He tried to choose a better feeling, recalling the monk's teachings about internal experience. For a few minutes, it worked. But as the line barely budged, frustration crept back in, stronger this time.

By the time they'd been waiting for 40 minutes, his shoulders were tense, and he was tapping his foot restlessly. The announcement came, cutting through the noise of the terminal: "Attention, passengers. Flight 102 to Mumbai is delayed by 90 minutes. We apologise for the inconvenience."

A collective groan rippled through the crowd. People scattered, rushing to find seats. Harrison's heart sank, and he felt a wave of irritation and fatigue wash over him.

They found a place to sit again, and Harrison collapsed into his chair with a heavy sigh. Around them, passengers muttered complaints, checked their phones, or leaned back in resigned frustration. The monk, as always, seemed unaffected.

"I know I'm supposed to be in charge of my internal experience," Harrison said, "but I can't seem to shake this. I'm tired, I'm frustrated, and I just can't feel good right now. How do you cope?"

The monk regarded him with quiet compassion. "Right now, you're suffering. I can see it clearly. But you must understand something: suffering is not real."

Harrison frowned. "What do you mean, not real? Of course, it's real. I'm feeling it right now. Everyone is."

"Pain is real and bad things do happen, but suffering them is a choice," the monk replied. "Suffering the situation is a choice."

Harrison stared at him, his mind processing this. Something about the monk's words struck a chord. He paused, observing his own state—the tension in his shoulders, the tightness in his chest, the restless energy. Then, suddenly, he saw it.

"I'm creating this," he realised. "I'm holding onto the frustration, the tension. I'm choosing to suffer this situation."

The moment he recognised it, the tension began to melt away.

"Wow. The second I noticed I was making myself feel bad, I stopped."

The monk smiled gently. "Exactly. When you consciously see that it's your choice, you naturally choose not to. Our lives can be effortless, but we create so much internal friction. Stress is internal friction. Suffering is internal friction."

Harrison leaned back, letting the monk's words settle over him. He consciously let go of all the frustration he'd been carrying, feeling the tightness in his body dissolve.

Harrison tilted his head, a new thought forming. "But what about waiting for long periods? I can manage for a little while, but after a few minutes, it gets harder."

The monk nodded, as though expecting the question.

"Understanding is needed. People suffer while waiting because they want reality to be different from what it is. They want to be elsewhere, to have the waiting end. But this is madness, because it can't possibly be. Reality is as it is. The key is to stop wanting to be somewhere else and to enjoy being here."

"So, acceptance?"

"Exactly. Acceptance brings peace. When you accept the moment as it is, without wishing it to be different, peace arises naturally."

Harrison's mind buzzed with this logic. It made perfect sense. He shifted in his chair, allowing himself to truly sit in the moment. The sounds of the terminal, the people passing by, even the waiting—all of it suddenly felt okay.

For the first time in years, he realised he had nothing to do. Nowhere to be. No one to please. And it felt amazing. He leaned back in his chair, observing the scene around him with a sense of ease.

"I've spent so much of my life rushing, planning, pushing forward," he thought to himself. "But right now, I have nothing to do but sit and be. And it's wonderful."

The 90 minutes passed quickly. He found himself enjoying the time, even smiling at the passengers around him as they prepared to board. When it was time to queue again, he felt no irritation—just a quiet acceptance of the process.

On the plane, the seats were small, and the cabin was crowded, but he felt no discomfort. He noticed how others around him fidgeted, sighed, and checked the time repeatedly. Many were clearly wishing the flight would end as soon as possible.

However, he now saw it differently.

"Why would I wish these nine hours away?" he thought to himself. "Life is so short—why would I wish any minute of it to be gone?"

He settled into his seat, observing the people around him, the hum of the plane, and the gentle sway of the cabin. For the entire flight, he maintained this perspective, feeling calm and content.

The hum of the plane's engines filled the cabin as Harrison sat back in his seat, a small notebook balanced on his lap. Around him, passengers fidgeted, adjusted their seats, and scrolled through their phones, trying to pass the time. Harrison, however, felt no rush, no discomfort. For the first time in years, he was happy just being simply present.

He flipped to a fresh page in his notebook, his pen hovering over the blank space. After a moment, he began to write, his thoughts flowing freely as he reflected on what he'd just learned.

The Nature of Suffering "Suffering is not real. Pain and discomfort exist, but suffering them is a choice. Suffering is the tension, frustration, and resistance we create within ourselves. When I realised I was choosing to suffer, I could stop. This is internal friction, and letting go of it makes life effortless."

The Importance of Acceptance "People suffer while waiting or enduring discomfort because they want reality to be different from what it is. This creates frustration, because it's impossible. Acceptance is the key—accepting the moment as it is brings peace. When I stopped wanting to be somewhere else, I could enjoy simply being here."

Reclaiming Time "Why would I wish time away? Life is short—every moment is precious, even the ones we think of as boring or uncomfortable. By staying present and appreciating the moment, I can reclaim time instead of wishing it away."

Effortless Living "Our lives are filled with unnecessary internal friction—stress, tension, and resistance. Letting go of this friction not only brings peace but also saves energy. Living effortlessly doesn't mean being lazy; it means moving through life without creating unnecessary struggle."

He leaned back, rereading what he'd written. The monk's teachings had shifted something profound within him. For years, he'd been trapped in cycles of frustration and striving, always rushing toward the next thing, never satisfied with the present. Now, for the first time, he saw another way.

He added one final note to the page: "Suffering is optional. Peace is possible. It's all about perspective."

As he closed the notebook and tucked it back into his bag, he felt a quiet sense of accomplishment. Not the kind that came from achieving something external, but the kind that came from within—an understanding, a shift, a step forward on the journey.

Looking out the window at the endless expanse of clouds, he smiled to himself. He was still learning, still growing, but he knew he was on the right path.

Chapter Eleven

Welcome to India

The plane touched down in Mumbai, the vibrant city already buzzing with life as the afternoon sun cast a golden glow over the bustling streets, reflecting off the glass facades of towering skyscrapers and illuminating the chaotic dance of rickshaws, taxis, and pedestrians below.

Despite the long flight, Harrison felt surprisingly refreshed. The yoga, meditation, and peaceful mindset cultivated during the journey had left him recharged.

At the arrivals terminal, they were met by a young monk, Kiran. Barely twenty, Kiran had a bright, youthful energy that immediately warmed Harrison. His saffron robes seemed oddly not out of place in the chaos of the airport, but his calm demeanour stood in sharp contrast to the bustling crowds around him.

"It is an honour to meet you," he said, his eyes shining. "Welcome to Mumbai. I will be your guide today."

He gestured toward a waiting rickshaw, its bright yellow and green exterior standing out among the sea of vehicles.

"This is my first time in India," Harrison said. "I can already tell it's going to be an adventure."

"Mumbai is unlike anywhere else. Let's start with a tour of the city before we settle in for the night."

The rickshaw zipped through the chaotic streets of Mumbai, Harrison holding on tightly as the driver expertly weaved between buses, cars, motorcycles, and even the occasional ox cart. Honks and shouts filled the air, not in anger, but as a kind of unspoken language of the road.

"The traffic is crazy!" he said, half in awe, half in terror.

Kiran laughed, clearly at ease. "This is Mumbai—chaos with a smile. It's a city where life is lived fully, no matter what."

As they sped through the streets, Harrison was mesmerised by the sheer vibrancy of the city:

Vendors selling everything from spices to phone chargers on bustling street corners. The aroma of street food wafting through the air—pav bhaji, vada pav, and sizzling kebabs. People in a kaleidoscope of colours, bustling along the pavements, each with a purpose and a smile

They caught a glimpse of the Haji Ali Dargah, a striking mosque and tomb set against the sea, connected to the mainland by a narrow causeway. Its white domes and minarets gleamed in the sunlight, a testament to Mumbai's diverse cultural heritage.

"This place is incredible," Harrison said. "It feels alive in a way I've never experienced before."

They arrived at a small, simple hotel tucked away in a quieter part of the city. The owner, Ramesh, greeted them with a wide grin and a deep bow.

"Welcome, sir! We are honoured to have you here. Please, make yourself at home."

Despite the modest accommodations, he felt a genuine warmth in Ramesh's welcome. The room was small but clean, with a comfortable bed and a ceiling fan that hummed softly.

"It's not luxurious, but it's perfect," Harrison thought to himself. "Simple, welcoming and real."

After dropping off their bags and freshening up, Kiran and Harrison set out for a tour of the city.

Kiran's excitement was infectious as he pointed out landmarks and shared stories about his hometown. They stopped by the Gateway of India, the grand arch overlooking the Arabian Sea. Built during British rule, it stood as a symbol of Mumbai's rich history.

From there, they wandered along Marine Drive, the famous promenade curving along the coastline. Harrison marvelled at the juxtaposition of modern skyscrapers and old colonial buildings.

Kiran insisted they try some street food, and Harrison hesitated only briefly before taking a bite of a spicy vada pav, Mumbai's beloved vegetarian street burger.

"This is amazing!" Harrison exclaimed. "Why haven't I tried this before?"

As the evening approached, they made their way to Juhu Beach, where the golden sand met the calm waves of the Arabian Sea. Harrison took in the scene: Families relaxing together, couples strolling hand in hand, and children laughing as they played games on the sand.

A group of boys kicked around a football, their laughter carrying over the sound of the waves.

"Do you think they'd let us join?" Harrison asked.

"Of course. Come on!"

The boys welcomed them eagerly, their energy boundless. Though Harrison was no match for their skill, he loved every moment of the game, diving into the joy and camaraderie. Kiran, barefoot and grinning, played with a natural ease that impressed everyone.

After the game, they walked to a small beachside restaurant, the lights twinkling as the sun dipped below the horizon. Harrison ordered a cold lime soda, savouring the refreshing sweetness as they sat and watched the waves.

As they relaxed, Harrison turned to Kiran.

"You said you grew up in Mumbai. What was that like?"

Kiran smiled, his gaze distant. "I was an orphan. I grew up in an orphanage in the city, surrounded by chaos but also by life. When I was fifteen, I met the monk. He came to the orphanage, teaching us about peace, happiness, and inner strength."

Harrison leaned forward, captivated. "And you decided to join him?"

"Not immediately. But his teachings stayed with me. I realised I wanted more than just survival—I wanted to grow, to understand myself and the world. So I joined him. That was five years ago, and it's been a process ever since. Happiness doesn't come overnight—it's something we cultivate, bit by bit. But coming from so little, I find the practice of gratitude and appreciation a very natural process. It brings me so much joy."

Harrison nodded, his respect for the young monk deepening, and he was eager to expand his own sense of joy.

As they returned to the hotel, Harrison reflected on the day. Mumbai had overwhelmed his senses, but it had also opened his heart. The warmth of the people, the vibrant energy of the city, and the joy of unexpected moments—these had made the chaos feel alive rather than daunting.

He fell asleep easily that night, the sound of distant traffic a comforting reminder of the city's unending heartbeat.

Chapter Twelve

Freedom from Identity

The first rays of sunlight crept through the window, illuminating the modest hotel room. Harrison stirred, expecting to reach for his phone as he always did. But something had changed. Instead of grabbing for his lifeline to the world, he smiled and pushed the covers back. Walking to the window, he took in the view.

Mumbai was alive with its unique rhythm, even in the early hours. The streets were already bustling, the honks of rickshaws blending with the chatter of vendors setting up their stalls. The city exuded energy, a harmony of chaos and life. He stood there for a moment, just breathing it in, noticing the peace in the simplicity of a new day.

Rolling out his mat, he began his morning practice. Each stretch felt more fluid, each breath longer and deeper. He marvelled at how his body, despite the long journey, seemed loose and alive. Yoga, he realised, wasn't just about flexibility—it was a daily reset, erasing tension and allowing him to begin anew.

The smell of spices and freshly brewed coffee greeted him as he descended to the dining area. Ramesh, ever the gracious host, welcomed him warmly.

"Good morning, sir. Did you sleep well?"

"I did, thank you. The room was perfect."

Ramesh guided him to the buffet, and Harrison's eyes widened at the spread. There were colourful fruits, steaming idlis, crisp dosas, and a chef ready to whip up an omelette to order. He filled his plate, savouring each bite, the mix of flavours a revelation.

With a cup of coffee in hand, he finally switched on his phone. The screen lit up with notifications: emails, messages, and social media alerts. He started with his emails, skimming through updates and replying to a few. Then came a message from his accountant—a reminder to start preparing his accounts for the year.

"I've still got three months, but I hate this part of the job," he thought to himself. The thought lingered, a dull worry settling in his chest.

Deciding to distract himself, he opened social media. Sharing a few pictures from Mumbai, he posted an update about his adventure, teasing his followers with the promise of a new book. The likes and comments began to trickle in, bringing a small buzz of satisfaction.

But as he scrolled through his feed, twenty minutes slipped away unnoticed. He grabbed another coffee, returning to his emails. That's when he saw it—an email notification about a one-star review for his business.

His heart sank. He opened the review, reading the harsh words that cut through the buzz of his morning.

"This is terrible," he thought to himself. "My rating will drop. What if I lose clients? I'm supposed to be on this journey, and my business is falling apart!"

The frustration mounted as doubts crept in. Was this the right time to leave? Could he afford to focus on self-discovery while his career wavered? He felt restless, his thoughts spiralling.

When the monks returned, their presence instantly calmed him. Harrison didn't hesitate to share his concerns, laying bare his frustrations and fears. The monk listened patiently, his eyes filled with understanding.

The monk's gaze was calm and steady as he began to speak. "You feel under threat because you believe your life is under threat. This is common. It stems from your identity."

Harrison frowned, trying to grasp the monk's words. "My identity? What does that have to do with it?"

"You believe you are something you are not. Our minds create strong identities—constructs of who we think we are. If we believe we are our minds, we can never truly be okay."

Harrison shook his head, confused. "I don't understand. It feels like my mind is all that I am. If I'm not my mind, then who am I?"

The monk smiled gently. "Your mind is a wonderful tool, but it is not you. Your mind is an accumulation of every experience, every situation you've been exposed to. It is constantly changing, shaped by what it consumes. But let's explore this further—who do you think you are, how would you describe yourself?"

"I am Harrison Marshall, a successful author and coach."

The monk's voice remained steady, guiding him. "You believe you are your name? But your name is just a sound your parents liked. It's not you."

Harrison chuckled, a surprising sense of relief washing over him. "I've always been particular about people pronouncing my name correctly. But now it seems funny—it is just a sound!"

"Next you described yourself as a successful author and coach, so you're defining yourself as your work. You believe your work is part of you, not only that, you believe success is part of you. Defining yourself as successful puts you under huge pressure to succeed constantly."

"Wow, I can see this does create a lot of pressure."

"Exactly. What else? Do you own a home?"

"Yes."

"Ownership is a societal construct. It helps make society function, but you must understand the land isn't truly yours. You must understand what's real—it's part of the earth."

Harrison nodded, the weight of the concept sinking in.

"Your identity also includes your money, your possessions, your country, your politics, your social media profiles, your family, your friends—even your favourite sports team. Each of these brings rules and expectations, and when any of them are threatened, you feel threatened."

Harrison's brows furrowed as the realisation dawned on him.

"If you believe you are so many things, you will live in constant jeopardy, because at any given moment, at least one of these aspects of your identity will be under threat."

The monk smiled gently, his tone soft yet firm. "Let's take your car as an example. How would you feel if your car were stolen?"

"I'd feel really bad—violated, frustrated, and angry at the thieves. Plus, it would cost me money and time to fix the situation."

The monk smiled knowingly. "That is a lot of suffering. But tell me—what is the benefit of all that suffering for you?"

Harrison blinked, the shift in perspective hitting him like a revelation. "Wow. I've never thought about it like that. I guess there's no benefit to it. It's bad enough losing the car—why would I make it worse by making myself suffer?"

The monk's smile deepened. "Exactly. The same applies to your work. Your work is not you. Letting go doesn't mean neglecting it—it means freeing yourself from unnecessary suffering."

Harrison sat in thoughtful silence before speaking again. "That's so powerful. But I still feel like I have such a large identity. Will that just fade on its own?"

"You need to keep digging into what's real and what's not. Examine each part of your identity. If it's a false belief that doesn't serve you, reject it. One by one, you will get closer to the reality of who you truly are."

He sat back, feeling lighter, freer. For the first time, he saw his identity not as a fixed reality, but as a collection of constructs he could question, release, and reshape.

As they prepared to leave, the monk placed a hand on Harrison's shoulder. "You are on the right path. On the next part of your journey, Kiran will guide you. We will meet again at the monastery."

Harrison smiled, bowing his head deeply in gratitude. "Thank you," he said sincerely. He found he had so much trust for the monk that this didn't seem like a big shift, just another part of the adventure.

The monk also bowed deeply, a gesture filled with reverence and care, before slowly walking away.

Kiran smiled warmly at Harrison. "Ready for the next leg of the journey?"

Harrison stood, his heart light, the path ahead clear.

Chapter Thirteen

The Train Adventure

The morning sun bathed Mumbai's Chhatrapati Shivaji Maharaj Terminus in golden light, highlighting its Gothic architecture as a testament to the city's historic grandeur. Harrison, his backpack slung over one shoulder, stood beside Kiran, who was brimming with enthusiasm.

"Are you ready for an adventure?" Kiran asked.

Harrison grinned. "Absolutely. I've handled the London underground at rush hour—how bad can it be?"

Kiran chuckled softly. "Indian railways unreserved compartment is a whole different world. You'll see."

Before entering the station, Kiran guided him to a bustling market to pick up provisions for the journey.

The market was a whirlwind of colours, sounds, and scents. Vendors called out their wares, their stalls laden with everything from ripe mangoes to spicy samosas. Harrison marvelled at the variety, allowing Kiran to take the lead.

"We'll need snacks that can last the journey. Let's start with some fruit."

They selected bananas, their golden skins promising a burst of energy, and oranges for their refreshing juice. Then came the savoury items: vada pav, they had enjoyed the day before, neatly wrapped in paper for easy transport. They also picked up samosas, flaky pastries stuffed with spiced potatoes, and a packet of namkeen, a savoury trail mix of fried lentils, nuts, and spices.

For sweets, Kiran insisted on jalebis, spirals of deep-fried dough soaked in syrup, and ladoos, sweet balls made of gram flour and sugar.

Finally, Kiran bought a thermos of chai, its aroma rich with ginger and cardamom.

"This is a feast!" Harrison exclaimed. "I'm not sure I can eat all of this."

"Don't worry. The train journey is long, and it is not all for us."

Back at the station, they navigated through the crowds, Harrison marvelling at the sheer scale of the place. Trains rumbled in and out of platforms, porters carried luggage balanced on their heads, and announcements echoed overhead in multiple languages.

They boarded their train early and managed to secure a bench in the unreserved compartment. Harrison noticed how the atmosphere was already lively, with families chatting and children playing games on the floor.

As departure time approached, the train grew increasingly crowded. The platform buzzed with urgency as families hugged goodbye, vendors shouted their final offers of snacks and tea, and porters hurried along with heavy luggage balanced on their heads.

As it pulled away, people were still jumping aboard, clutching onto railings and squeezing through open doors while others hoisted friends and family members up from the moving platform. The rhythmic clatter of the wheels on the tracks began to settle into a steady hum, and the chaotic energy of departure gave way to a quiet acceptance of the long journey ahead.

At each stop, more passengers climbed aboard, filling every inch of space. Harrison observed something remarkable: younger men and women giving up their seats for the elderly, women, and children without hesitation. Despite the crowd and lack of personal space, there was an unspoken harmony among the passengers—a collective understanding that they were all in this together. Harrison felt humbled by their patience, resilience, and kindness amid the packed compartments and stifling heat.

"This level of care and community is incredible," he thought to himself. "It happens sometimes in London, but not like this."

By the third stop, the train was packed, and the atmosphere was a cacophony of conversations, laughter, and the occasional cry of a vendor selling tea or snacks. When an old man entered at the second stop, both Kiran and Harrison stood to offer their seats.

The man accepted with a smile, pressing his palms together in a gesture of gratitude.

"There's something special about this," Harrison thought to himself. "It feels... human. Like we're all looking out for each other."

By the fourth stop, the train seemed impossibly full. Yet more passengers poured in, finding space in the narrow aisles or even hanging off the sides. Harrison's jaw dropped as he saw several men climbing onto the roof.

"They're climbing the roof?!"

Kiran nodded with a smile. "It's common. The men take the roof to make space for women, children, and the elderly inside. Despite all the discomfort, you'll notice they're still smiling. Life isn't easy for many of these people, but they don't lose their enthusiasm."

One of the men on the roof leaned down, extending a hand to help others up. Kiran turned to Harrison.

"Would you like to try? It's an experience you won't forget."

Harrison hesitated, then grinned. "Why not? It'll also free up more space inside."

Kiran gestured to one of the roof-climbers, who swung his arm down. Another man held him steady, and with Kiran's help, Harrison climbed onto the man's shoulders and swung himself up.

Once on the roof, Kiran followed with practised ease, pulling himself up in a single fluid motion. Harrison found himself sitting cross-legged alongside dozens of other men, the wind rushing past as the train began to move.

The view was breathtaking. As the city faded behind them, fields of green stretched out on either side, dotted with small villages and distant hills. The wind whipped through his hair, and he felt a sense of freedom he hadn't known in years.

"This is incredible," Harrison thought to himself. "I've never felt so alive."

Kiran pointed out landmarks as they passed—a distant temple spire, a small lake glittering in the sunlight, farmers working in the fields.

The camaraderie on the roof was infectious. The men shared snacks, chatted, and laughed, making room for each new climber at the next stop. One man, Raj, pulled out a harmonium, playing a lively tune that had everyone clapping along.

As night fell, the stars emerged, brilliant against the inky sky. Harrison leaned back, gazing up, feeling a deep sense of contentment.

"This is what an adventure feels like," he thought to himself. "Not just seeing new places, but experiencing life in a way I never imagined."

Kiran smiled, as though sensing his thoughts. "How's the view?"

"Unreal. Thank you for bringing me here."

The train chugged along, its rhythm steady, carrying them closer to the next leg of their journey. For Harrison, the night on the roof of the train was a moment he would carry with him forever—a reminder of the joy and resilience of life.

As the train approached Mathura, Harrison felt a surge of anticipation. Kiran, sensing his excitement, leaned in with a smile.

"Mathura is not just a city," Kiran explained. "It's the birthplace of Lord Krishna, a place where divinity and history intertwine."

The train slowed to a halt at Mathura Junction, and the duo disembarked into the bustling station. The air was thick with the aroma of street food and the sounds of vendors calling out their wares. Navigating through the crowd, they made their way to the exit.

As they stepped outside, a familiar voice called out. It was Raj, the man they had met on the train roof.

"Welcome to Mathura!" he called. "I hope you enjoyed the ride."

"It was unforgettable, Raj. Thank you for your hospitality."

"If you don't have plans for the night, my family and I would be honoured to host you. Our home is humble, but our hearts are big."

Harrison glanced at Kiran, who nodded approvingly.

"We would be delighted, Raj. Thank you."

They followed Raj through the narrow, winding streets of Mathura. The city's vibrant energy was palpable—children playing, vendors selling colourful trinkets, and the occasional cow meandering through the lanes. Harrison marvelled at the intricate carvings on ancient temples and the harmonious blend of old and new.

Arriving at Raj's home, they were greeted by his wife, Meera, and their two children. The small house exuded warmth, with the aroma of spices wafting from the kitchen.

"Please, make yourselves at home," Meera said. "Dinner will be ready soon."

They sat on woven mats in the cosy living area, sharing stories and laughter. Despite their modest means, Raj's family radiated joy and generosity.

Before the meal, Raj suggested a visit to the Sri Krishna Janmabhoomi Temple, the birthplace of Lord Krishna.

"It's a short walk from here, and it's especially serene at night."

The group strolled through the moonlit streets, the city's daytime hustle giving way to a tranquil ambiance. Reaching the temple complex, Harrison was struck by its grandeur and spiritual aura. The main shrine stood majestically, adorned with intricate carvings depicting scenes from Krishna's life.

Inside, the air was filled with the soft chants of devotees and the gentle glow of oil lamps. The calm sense of peace was infectious, and Harrison felt humbled and connected to the place.

"This is where Lord Krishna was born, over five thousand years ago," Kiran explained softly. "It's a place of immense spiritual significance."

Harrison closed his eyes, absorbing the sanctity of the moment. He felt a deep connection to the stories Kiran had shared, the teachings of the monk, and the journey that had led him here.

After offering their respects, they returned to Raj's home, bringing with them a new calmer, more humble atmosphere.

After a hearty meal of dal, chapati, and sabzi, Harrison sat with Raj on the woven mats, sipping a steaming cup of chai. He savoured the warmth of the tea, the rich depth of the flavour, and soaked in the hospitality he'd experienced throughout the evening.

Raj's children giggled in a corner, playing with wooden toys, while Meera cleaned up in the kitchen, humming softly.

He leaned back, gazing at Raj with a mix of gratitude and curiosity.

"Raj, I have to ask," Harrison began. "How can you give so much? Back home, this level of generosity isn't common. People tend to hold tightly to what they have."

Raj paused, his kind eyes reflecting both wisdom and humility. He set his cup down, the corners of his mouth lifting in a small smile.

"I understand why you would feel that way," Raj said thoughtfully. "But here in India, there is an underlying understanding of life. It's not something written in books or taught in schools—it's something we grow up feeling, learning from our yogis, monks, our temples, and our stories. This understanding is that we are all one."

Harrison tilted his head, intrigued. "One? You mean, like... connected?"

"More than connected. We are not separate at all. We are all part of life, part of the same big family. There is no such thing as an individual. What we do for others, we do for ourselves. When you eat, I eat. When you smile, I smile."

Harrison paused, trying to grasp the idea. "But surely there's a limit? I mean, don't you have to look out for yourself and your family first?"

Raj chuckled, shaking his head. "You see, that's where the misunderstanding begins. When a beggar knocks at my door, it's not 'my' food that I give him. It is 'our' food. This home, this meal, it doesn't belong to me. It belongs to life, to us all."

Harrison stared into his cup, Raj's words stirring something deep within him. He thought of the life he'd left behind—the relentless pursuit of success, the walls he'd built to protect his own interests.

"That's so different from the way I was raised," Harrison reflected. "Back home, people are focused on the individual—your career, your achievements, your possessions. Everything is about what you can earn and keep for yourself."

Raj nodded, his expression thoughtful. "That way of thinking creates separation. It's a kind of loneliness, isn't it? Always trying to hold on, to protect what you have. Here, we understand that we are part of something much bigger. When you live with that awareness, there is no fear of losing, because there is nothing to lose. And there is no pride in giving, because it's not yours to give. It's simply what must be done."

Harrison felt a wave of emotion—gratitude, awe, and a sense of freedom he hadn't known before. He looked around the room at Raj's family, their modest home filled with love and laughter despite its simplicity.

"It's incredible. I've spent so much of my life trying to protect what I thought was mine. But hearing you say it, I can see how that way of thinking is isolating."

Raj placed a hand on Harrison's shoulder, his voice gentle. "You're here now. And you are part of our family. Tonight, this food, this home—it is yours, too."

Harrison smiled, a sense of belonging washing over him. "Thank you, Raj. For everything. I'll never forget this."

"No thanks are needed. You are not a guest. You are family."

Later that night, lying on a simple cot, Harrison stared at the ceiling, replaying Raj's words in his mind.

"We are all one," he thought to himself. "There's no such thing as mine or yours, only ours. It's such a simple idea, but it changes everything. With this understanding, I could feel like everyone was part of my family and I am part of theirs. There is so much love and connectedness that comes from family, to live like this would be wonderful."

He thought of how differently he might approach his own life with this understanding. His work, his relationships, even the way he viewed success—it all seemed ripe for re-examination.

As he drifted to sleep, he felt a profound sense of peace, knowing that he was part of something greater than himself.

Chapter Fourteen

Journey to Rishikesh

Harrison awoke early, feeling refreshed and clear-headed. The soft light of dawn spilled into the room, turning the edges of his mat golden as he unrolled it on the floor. His breath moved in harmony with each stretch—slow, deliberate, and cleansing.

With every movement, tension melted away. His body opened, and his mind stilled. By the time he finished his practice, he sat in a peaceful stillness, feeling as though his body and mind had been reset.

"Every day starts fresh, like I'm a new person," he thought to himself. "My body and mind—cleansed completely."

It was an incredible feeling. How had he lived for so long without this kind of clarity?

The Journey Begins

Kiran, Aarav, and Harrison gathered their belongings and headed to the train station. Aarav—Raj's son—was joining them to begin his role as a trainee teacher at a yoga school in Rishikesh. Despite his youth, Aarav carried himself with quiet confidence, his determination evident but gentle, like a steady flame.

The station buzzed with life—vendors calling out, trains rumbling, and crowds of travellers moving in every direction. This time, they managed to secure seats in a reserved cabin. Harrison sighed in gratitude as he settled in.

"Let me grab us some coffee. It's a long trip," he said, standing as the train pulled away from the platform.

Kiran smiled, serene as ever. "None for me, thank you."

"Just water for me, if you see a vendor," Aarav added politely.

Harrison returned with an extra-strong coffee for himself, its rich aroma filling the cabin. He took a sip, feeling the familiar rush of energy spread through him. The hum of the train and the rhythmic clatter of its wheels added to his excitement.

The train had settled into its pace, winding its way through the countryside. Harrison turned to Aarav, his caffeine-fuelled enthusiasm bubbling over.

"So, Aarav, you're teaching yoga. That's fantastic. What's your long-term goal?"

Aarav smiled softly, his gaze steady. "One day, I'd like to become the main teacher at a school. To earn enough to support a small family and live a simple, happy life."

Harrison really wanted to help young Aarav, to return the hospitality from last night—this was what he was good at, success and business. He was excited, and the buzz in his veins quickly took over. Leaning forward, his voice quickened with energy.

"That's great, Aarav. But why stop there? With the right strategy, you could have your own school within a year. Think about it—branding, online classes, expanding your reach. You could go global. You've got so much potential!"

The ideas poured out of him, unstoppable. He outlined business plans, marketing strategies, and ways to scale. His heart raced, his mind spinning with possibilities.

Aarav listened patiently, not interrupting, his calm a stark contrast to Harrison's growing excitement. When Harrison finally paused, Aarav spoke gently.

"I really appreciate your ideas and your help. But I can't open my own school yet. I have much to learn. I need to master inner peace for myself before I can teach it to others, and this will take time and focus."

The words landed like a thunderclap. Harrison sat back, stunned.

"So many teachers in the West teach things they haven't mastered themselves," he thought. "But Aarav knows better. Mastery must come first."

As the realisation settled, Harrison noticed his own state—his heart still racing, his mind buzzing. Despite all his morning practice, here he was again: restless and unbalanced.

"Why is this happening?" he asked. "I do my daily practice, but I'm still getting stressed and overexcited. Why can't I calm down?"

Kiran, who had been observing quietly, finally spoke. His voice was steady, filled with understanding.

"You need to understand karma. Every action—whether physical, spoken, or thought—creates momentum. Karma can be viewed simply as the momentum of action."

Harrison frowned. "So, it's like Newton's law? Every action has an equal and opposite reaction?"

"Exactly," Kiran nodded. "But it's not just cause and effect. Certain actions increase energy, and others calm it. Right now, you have a lot of energy and a tendency to become excitable. You don't need actions that add to this energy—you need actions that stabilise and calm you."

Harrison thought back to his morning: the extra-strong coffee, the burst of excitement while planning Aarav's school. Each action had built more and more energy, throwing him out of balance.

"Imagine your energy as a pendulum" Kiran continued, "swinging back and forth. Every action you take either swings it further or calms it toward stillness. Our goal is to reduce the swing until the pendulum remains steady at the centre—calm and at peace."

"I see it now," Harrison nodded. "My actions swung the pendulum too far. That's why I feel unbalanced."

Aarav chimed in softly, his voice filled with wisdom beyond his years. "Hatha Yoga teaches us about ha and tha—sun and moon. Some practices create heat and energy, while others are calming and cooling. Balance comes when you choose the actions that serve you in each moment."

Harrison pulled out his notebook, inspired to make a list. He divided the page into two columns and titled them:

Ha (Energy-Raising):

- Coffee, sugar
- Speaking excitedly
- Success
- Intense exercise

Tha (Energy-Calming):

- Tea
- Slow breathing
- Yoga
- Meditation
- Silence

"This is so simple, but so powerful," he thought to himself. "If I can balance these forces, I can maintain peace no matter what life throws at me."

As the train continued its journey, Harrison felt a wave of clarity wash over him. He looked out the window, watching the golden fields roll by under a soft sun. He turned to Kiran and Aarav, gratitude swelling within him.

"Thank you, both of you," he said. "This insight really helps me understand the effects of my actions. It's powerful."

Kiran smiled warmly. "The journey is about awareness. Step by step, you're finding your balance."

Leaning back into his seat, Harrison allowed himself to relax fully for the first time in hours. The pendulum within him was still swinging, but now he understood it. Now he knew how to bring it to rest. And with that understanding came a quiet, growing peace.

The train journey to Rishikesh felt unlike any other. Seated with Kiran and Aarav, Harrison found himself mesmerised by the scenery unfolding beyond the window. Fields stretched endlessly, interrupted by clusters of trees, and then forests. As the hours passed, the first faint outlines of the Himalayas emerged on the distant horizon, their jagged peaks rising like silent sentinels.

The gentle rocking of the train, the rhythmic clatter of wheels on the tracks, and the easy, natural flow of conversation with his companions lulled Harrison into a state of peaceful awareness. He relaxed, letting the moment settle around him.

After a while, he pulled out his notebook again. Writing had always been his way of grounding himself, of capturing what he felt but couldn't yet articulate.

"Travelling has a way of bringing us into the present," he wrote. "In new places, we shed expectations—because we have none. Everything feels fresh, surprising, alive. It's easy to appreciate new sights, sounds, and smells when we see them for the first time. But how can I cultivate this beginner's mind in the familiar? The monk's words on expectations echo in my thoughts: the less we expect, the more we can truly see and savour life."

He paused, gazing out at the rolling fields and imagining a traveller in England marvelling at the same sights he once took for granted.

"Maybe it's not about the place," he thought to himself. "It's about the mindset. A beginner's mind can find beauty anywhere."

He paused, watching as the landscape shifted again. Forests thinned out, and small towns rolled by, punctuated with flashes of colour—women in bright saris, market stalls bursting with fresh produce, and vibrant murals on ancient walls.

Chapter Fifteen

Welcome to Rishikesh

With each passing mile, the Himalayas grew, then as the train began its final approach, the scene outside changed dramatically. The first clear glimpse of the Ganges emerged, its blue-green waters shimmering under the sunlight. The sight stopped Harrison mid-thought.

"Wow..." he whispered.

The river was breathtaking. He'd heard countless negative stories about how polluted the Ganges was downstream, but this—this was pristine, vibrant, and alive. It flowed with a quiet power, snaking its way through the foothills of the Himalayas like a ribbon of blue light.

Stepping off the train, he was immediately struck by the change in atmosphere. Rishikesh had a calm yet vibrant energy, buzzing with life but in a way that felt serene and unhurried.

The city stretched along both sides of the Ganges, the crystal-clear water flowing through its heart. Temples and ashrams lined the banks, their white and ochre spires reaching toward the sky. Bells rang faintly in the distance, mingling with the soft hum of chanting that seemed to rise from the very stones of the place.

"Welcome to Rishikesh, the yoga capital of the world," Kiran smiled. "It's a sacred city—vegetarian, alcohol-free, and no cars are allowed in the main area. This helps preserve its spiritual environment."

"Wow, I feel so drawn to the Ganges... it's like it's calling to me. How about we go for a swim?"

Kiran and Aarav exchanged smiles, clearly pleased at Harrison's enthusiasm.

"An excellent idea, my friend," Aarav said. "There's nothing like it. The Ganges isn't just a river; it's a lifeline. It's seen as the bringer of life, flowing straight from the Himalayas—the very source of purity and energy."

Harrison looked back at the river, captivated by its clarity. The blue-green water sparkled under the midday sun, its surface rippling gently. It was as if the river had a pulse, alive with an ancient, unspoken wisdom.

"For us, swimming in the Ganges is more than just a physical act," Aarav continued. "It's a connection—to the mountains where it begins, to the land it nourishes, to the life it sustains. It washes away more than dirt; it clears the mind, the body, and the spirit."

Harrison felt a strange excitement bubbling within him, like a child discovering something magical for the first time.

"It's incredible to think about..." he said softly. "This river flowing for thousands of miles, carrying the essence of the mountains. It feels... sacred."

"Because it is," Kiran smiled. "For millennia, people have come here to cleanse themselves—not just physically, but emotionally and spiritually. The water carries a purity that is more than what the eyes see. You'll feel it when you're in it."

As they walked, scooters zipped past on narrow pavements, and Harrison raised an eyebrow.

"I thought there were no vehicles here?"

Both Kiran and Aarav laughed.

"It's India," Kiran said. "There's always a flow of life, even in the most serene places."

Crossing the Ganges

They reached a large suspension bridge—Laxman Jhula, its iron frame swaying gently with the foot traffic. A cow blocked much of the path, contentedly chewing cud, while people calmly stepped around it.

"Cows are sacred here," Aarav explained, "symbols of life and nourishment. They're part of the family."

Harrison marvelled at how smoothly everyone navigated around the cow, their patience and reverence a stark contrast to the hustle he was used to back home. Monkeys perched on the railings, darting down to snatch treats from travellers. Below, enormous fish gathered in the river, snapping up offerings thrown by passers-by.

The trio made their way down to the riverbank. The path was alive with movement—pilgrims performing rituals, monks meditating, and children playing in the shallow edges of the water. Women in vibrant saris released small leaf bowls carrying flowers and candles into the river, their offerings gently drifting downstream.

Harrison watched in awe, absorbing the scene. There was a palpable reverence for the Ganges, a collective acknowledgement of its importance. He kicked off his shoes and rolled up his trousers, his feet sinking into the cool, smooth stones beneath the water.

"It's freezing!" he exclaimed. "But it feels... amazing."

Kiran and Aarav laughed as they waded deeper into the water. Aarav didn't hesitate; he plunged straight in, letting out a joyful whoop as the cold water embraced him. Kiran followed, his movements graceful and unhurried, as though he were merging with the river itself.

Harrison took a breath, his excitement mixed with a small hesitation. Then, gathering his courage, he dove in. The icy water hit him like a shock, and for a moment, everything fell silent. His breath caught, his skin tingled, and every thought evaporated.

When he surfaced, gasping but grinning, he felt a jolt of energy course through him—something vibrant, cleansing, and completely alive.

"This is incredible!" Harrison laughed. "It's like the river wakes up every cell in my body."

Aarav floated nearby, his face serene. "It does. It wakes you up. It connects you to something far greater than yourself. You can feel it, can't you?"

Harrison nodded, unable to find the words. Floating in the cold, clear water, he felt stripped of all the noise, the tension, the expectations. The current pulled gently at him, and for the first time in a long time, he allowed himself to simply let go.

The three of them floated, swam, and laughed, splashing each other like carefree children. Time seemed to slow, the world beyond the river fading away.

Eventually, they waded back to the shore, the sun warming their skin as they lay on the smooth stones, letting the experience settle into their bones.

"The mountains, the river, the people..." Harrison whispered to himself. "It's all connected. It's all alive, and so am I."

Kiran turned to him, hearing his whisper. "Yes. And the more you let yourself feel this connection, the more life reveals itself to you."

Harrison closed his eyes, the sounds of the river and the distant chanting blending into a soothing symphony. He'd come to Rishikesh in search of something, and here, in the icy embrace of the Ganges, he felt he'd touched the edge of it.

They lay on the warm rocks, drying off under the sun. Harrison felt utterly content, drifting into a light sleep.

Chapter Sixteen

Evening in Rishikesh

Waking as the sun set, the group made their way back across the bridge to a riverside café with a panoramic view. Harrison, Kiran, and Aarav sat cross-legged at a low table, sipping ginger, lemon, and honey tea in silence. The golden light of dusk painted the Himalayan foothills, and the steady hum of the river below filled the air.

Nothing needed to be said. The shared stillness spoke volumes.

That evening, Aarav guided them to his yoga school, where they climbed to the rooftop dining area. The view stretched out over Rishikesh, the sun setting behind the hills, bathing the city in a warm, golden glow. The in-house chef had prepared a feast of vegetarian dishes—simple yet vibrant, each plate offering a symphony of colours and aromas.

The students sat in silence, savouring their food with deliberate focus. Harrison followed suit, matching their stillness and intention.

At first, it was easy to appreciate the meal. The subtle spices gave each mouthful such a depth of flavour, the freshness of the vegetables crisp with energy. Each bite felt new, surprising, and deeply satisfying.

But after a few mouthfuls, Harrison noticed his mind drifting. He began to eat out of habit, his focus slipping as he treated the meal like a task to complete.

"Why do I chase food, desire it so much, and then rush through eating it?" he thought to himself. "I treat it like a box to tick off a list, when it's one of the greatest pleasures life offers."

He paused, watching his thoughts unfold. The realisation struck him as he began to notice himself applying the new knowledge to real life.

"It's my expectations again. The first few bites felt wonderful because they were new. Then I assumed the next bite would taste the same, and I stopped paying attention. But how can two bites ever be the same? Each mouthful is unique if I'm truly here to experience it."

Taking a slow breath, Harrison picked up his fork again, this time with intention. He treated the next bite with a beginner's mind—as though he were tasting it for the very first time. He noticed the crunch of the vegetables, the delicate balance of spices, the richness of each flavour.

Suddenly, he was back—fully present, fully engaged. His appreciation deepened, and the meal transformed into something extraordinary.

"Wow," he thought, smiling to himself. "I was close to missing another meal. A simple act like eating can be a meditation, a training ground for awareness. The ability to be present and at peace is growing in me every day, with every small moment of practice."

The rooftop grew quieter as the light faded completely, leaving behind the soft hum of the river below. Harrison sat in silence, savouring the meal with gratitude, realising just how much richness there was in life when he slowed down enough to truly see it.

Later that night, the three companions climbed to the rooftop to watch the stars. The moon lit up the Himalayas, casting a silver glow over the temples by the river. They sat together, soaking in the tranquillity.

Harrison felt a deep connection to his companions. It was a feeling beyond words, a profound sense of belonging.

Chapter Seventy

The Journey to the Monastery

The next morning, Harrison awoke early. Despite the promise of a yoga session with Aarav, he began with his own daily practice. It was a commitment he had made to himself and the monk, and he wouldn't break it. By the time he finished, he felt deeply at peace.

In the studio, Aarav guided them through a session that stretched Harrison's body in new ways, introducing advanced poses and techniques. The real challenge, however, was the breathwork. They practised bellows breath (Bhastrika), skull-shining breath (Kapalabhati), and alternate nostril breathing (Nadi Shodhana). By the end, his mind was crystal clear, his body humming with energy.

As they prepared to leave, Aarav embraced Harrison, tears streaming down his face.

"Thank you for sharing this journey with me. May your path bring you peace."

Harrison, deeply moved, let his own emotions flow freely. "Thank you, Aarav. For your kindness, your wisdom, and your friendship."

With a packed lunch prepared by the chef, Harrison and Kiran set off for the next leg of their adventure, the warmth of Rishikesh lingering in their hearts.

The morning air in Rishikesh was crisp, carrying with it the faint scent of incense and the soft chiming of temple bells as the city stirred awake. They crossed the suspension bridge over the river, its gentle sway more pronounced in the calm of dawn. Below, the turquoise waters shimmered like liquid jewels, carrying whispers of their Himalayan source.

"Today, we have a long hike ahead of us," Kiran said. "The monastery is at a high altitude, and the journey will take all day."

Harrison felt a thrill of excitement mingled with apprehension. He was confident in his fitness—after all, he exercised regularly and prided himself on his strength. But something in Kiran's tone hinted at the challenge ahead, and he was learning to trust his judgement.

As they left the city behind, the paved roads gave way to dirt paths winding through dense forest. The trees stretched high above, their leaves creating a mosaic of dappled sunlight on the ground. Birds called to one another in the canopy, their songs blending with the rustling of the underbrush as small animals darted out of sight.

Kiran set a steady pace, his movements fluid and easy. Harrison matched him stride for stride, impressed by Kiran's energy.

"He can't exercise as much as me, but he climbs with such ease," Harrison thought to himself. "I'll keep up—it'll be a good challenge."

As the hours wore on, the trail grew steeper. The forest began to thin, revealing glimpses of the mountains ahead. Harrison's legs began to ache, a dull burn spreading through his thighs and calves. He glanced at Kiran, whose pace remained unbroken, his smile unchanged.

By mid-morning, the trees had thinned to scattered groves, and the path had turned rocky and uneven. Harrison's breathing grew heavier, his muscles tightening with each step. Sweat clung to his skin despite the cool air.

"I'm fit. I've trained for years. But this is hard," he thought. "How does he make it look so easy?"

Kiran, sensing Harrison's struggle, turned back with a warm smile. "We'll rest soon. Just around the next bend, there's a beautiful spot with a view."

The promise of rest pushed him forward. He focused on the trail ahead, willing his legs to carry him a little further. When they rounded the bend, the view took his breath away—a sweeping vista of the valley below, the Ganges snaking its way through the landscape, and the distant peaks rising like sentinels.

They sat on a flat rock, unpacking a simple breakfast of fruit and chapati, a homemade flatbread. Harrison collapsed with a sigh, grateful for the break. As they ate, he turned to Kiran, curiosity overcoming his fatigue.

"How are you so fit?" Harrison asked. "You must do an incredible amount of endurance training to hike like this with such ease."

Kiran chuckled softly. "It's not about fitness. The first time I climbed this path, I struggled just as you are now. I was no different. What changed was my awareness."

Harrison frowned, confused. "But my body feels tired. Isn't that just a physical limitation?"

Kiran smiled, his voice gentle but probing. "What is tired? Examine it for yourself."

Harrison paused, considering the question. "Tiredness is... fatigue, a lack of energy."

"And this lack of energy—does it mean you can't take another step? Or does it mean you're thinking about how far you have to go, how many steps you've already taken?"

Harrison blinked, the monk's words hitting him like a revelation.

"Only the next step is real," Kiran continued. "Pain is real, yes, but the pain you feel is not too much to bear. The tiredness you feel is not stopping you from taking another step. Your suffering comes from the weight of the future and the past. Let go of those, and see what's left."

Harrison closed his eyes, tuning into his body. He scanned for the fatigue he'd been carrying, but instead, he found himself surprisingly whole. His legs felt fine. His breathing was already steady.

"It's true," he thought to himself. "Right now, I'm fine. The suffering was all in my mind, a story I was telling myself."

When they resumed the hike, Harrison experimented with the monk's advice. Each step became its own moment, complete and independent of what came before or what lay ahead. The rhythm of his feet against the rocky path, the sound of his breath in the cool mountain air, the warmth of the sun on his back—all these sensations anchored him to the present.

The climb grew steeper, and the air thinner as they gained altitude. Snow began to appear in patches along the trail, glistening in the sunlight. Harrison marvelled at the stark beauty of the landscape—the rugged cliffs, the icy streams cutting through the rocks, and the vast sky stretching endlessly above.

He noticed Kiran moving ahead, his pace unchanged. But now, instead of striving to match him, Harrison focused only on his own steps, one at a time.

His legs still ached, and his muscles burned, but the weight of the climb had lifted. He felt lighter, freer, as though he had shed a burden he hadn't realised he was carrying.

At a particularly steep incline, Kiran paused, waiting for Harrison to catch up.

"I see it now," Harrison said. "My body isn't holding me back—it's my mind. I've been suffering the climb, not because it's hard, but because I've been thinking about how hard it is."

Kiran nodded, his smile serene. "Exactly. When you let go of suffering, you let go of the internal friction, the path becomes just a path. Each step becomes just a step. And you, my friend, become free."

They continued, Harrison now moving with a newfound ease. The mountain no longer loomed as an insurmountable challenge but unfolded step by step, moment by moment.

As they climbed higher, the dense greenery of the forest gave way to a more barren landscape. He noticed the first patches of snow dusting the trail and surrounding rocks. He paused, marvelling at the sight.

"Snow... on this incredible hike," he thought to himself. "What an adventure. I never imagined this journey would take me somewhere so wild and beautiful."

The snow was thin at first, a delicate veil over the earth. But as they ascended, it grew thicker, blanketing the ground and clinging to the rocks in shimmering layers.

Harrison continued to practise the monk's teachings. Each time he felt fatigue creeping in or his legs beginning to ache, he paused to scan his body. He let go of any internal resistance, reminding himself that suffering was a choice. The realisation never ceased to surprise him. His body, though tired, was perfectly capable of the task.

"It's just one step. And another. That's all that's real. Everything else is in my head."

As he let go of his internal struggle, he found a natural rhythm. His steps became lighter, his breath more even. He noticed the crunch of snow beneath his boots, the sharp chill of the mountain air, and the way the sunlight glinted off the icy surfaces around them. The climb transformed from a gruelling challenge to an exhilarating experience.

After another two hours of steady climbing, the path curved around a ridge. As they rounded the bend, Harrison's breath caught in his throat. In the distance, perched against the side of the mountain, stood the monastery.

The structure seemed to grow out of the rock itself, blending seamlessly with the landscape. Its centrepiece was a magnificent pyramid-shaped building, its golden roof glinting in the sunlight like a beacon. Around it, four smaller pyramids stood in perfect symmetry, their rooftops capped with snow.

The monastery's intricate carvings were faintly visible even from this distance—statues of deities and guardians etched into the stone walls, their forms weathered but imposing. A long flight of steep, snow-covered stairs led to the main entrance, framed by an ornate archway adorned with golden symbols.

Harrison stood in awe, taking in the sight. "It's breathtaking. Like it's always been here, part of the mountain. How did they even build something like this in such a remote place?"

Kiran placed a hand on his shoulder, his eyes serene. "This monastery is more than a place of training. It's a meeting point—where human effort and the divine come together. Each stone was carried here by hand, each carving a labour of devotion."

Harrison felt a deep sense of respect for the people who had created such a marvel. The monastery was magnificent, its golden rooftops gleaming against the stark white of the snow-covered mountain.

With the final stretch ahead, he tightened the straps of his pack, took a deep breath of the crisp mountain air, and stepped forward. For the first time, he noticed how tension had disappeared from his body. His movements felt effortless, his breathing steady. The challenge was still there, but it was no longer a source of suffering. Instead, it felt like a thrilling adventure, each step bringing him closer to something extraordinary.

"I'm not fighting the climb anymore," he thought to himself. "It's just... flowing. I can't believe how light I feel."

As they drew closer to the monastery, the golden rooftops seemed to glow even brighter, reflecting the late afternoon sun. The surrounding peaks loomed majestically, their rugged forms softened by layers of snow. The air grew colder, but he barely noticed. His focus was on the journey, the steady rhythm of his steps, and the sense of peace that filled him with each moment.

Kiran stopped briefly, turning with a knowing smile. "The hardest climbs lead to the most beautiful views. But remember—each step is as important as the destination. The monastery will wait for us."

Harrison nodded, his heart swelling with gratitude and excitement. The journey had already transformed him in ways he couldn't yet fully understand, and the monastery, standing proudly against the mountain, seemed to promise even more.

Chapter Eighteen

Arrival at the Monastery

The final steps of the ascent brought them to a wide, flat plateau where the monastery stood, majestic and serene. As Harrison approached the grand staircase leading to the entrance, a familiar figure emerged from the shadows of the stone archway—the monk who had first guided him on this journey.

The monk's face lit up with a warm smile as he walked forward to greet them.

"Welcome, my friend. And you too, Kiran. It brings me great joy to see you both here."

Harrison felt an overwhelming sense of relief and accomplishment. The sight of his old friend, standing before the magnificent monastery, filled him with gratitude.

"It's good to see you again," Harrison said. "And to finally reach this place—it feels like a dream."

The monk chuckled softly, patting him on the shoulder. "Come, let us leave the cold behind. You must be tired from your journey."

The monk guided them up the wide, snow-dusted steps. Harrison paused at the entrance, gazing up at the intricate carvings that adorned the archway. Scenes from ancient scriptures were etched into the stone, depicting deities, animals, and celestial patterns that seemed to tell stories older than time itself. Golden inlays shimmered in the fading light, giving the monastery an otherworldly glow.

Inside, the air was warmer, infused with the faint scent of incense. The floor was polished stone, cool beneath their feet. They stopped just beyond the threshold, where a simple wooden rack held neatly arranged slippers and sandals.

"Here, we leave our shoes," the monk explained. "The monastery is a sacred space, and we walk its halls barefoot to connect with the earth and ground ourselves."

Harrison bent down, removing his boots. The cool stone beneath his feet felt both grounding and humbling.

The monk led them to a large central chamber where a fire crackled in a stone hearth. The room was sparse yet inviting, its walls adorned with murals of mountain landscapes and ancient sages in meditation. Low cushions surrounded the fire, and Harrison gratefully sank onto one, feeling the warmth seep into his chilled body.

A young monk appeared silently, carrying a tray with steaming cups of ginger and honey tea. He placed the tray before them with a small bow before retreating as quietly as he had come.

Harrison wrapped his hands around the warm cup, inhaling the comforting aroma. As he sipped, he welcomed the heat, warming him from the inside out.

They sat in companionable silence for a while, gazing out through an open window at the valley below. The snow-covered peaks glowed faintly in the twilight, and the distant sound of wind was the only noise.

The monk turned to Harrison, his eyes gleaming with gentle curiosity.

"How was your journey? I can see already that you have begun to master your body and mind."

Harrison smiled, setting his cup down. "It was challenging, but... transformative. At first, I struggled. I thought my body was holding me back, but Kiran explained—it wasn't my body at all. It was my mind. The more I let go of resistance, the easier the climb became. Each step was just a step, nothing more. It's strange—by the end, I wasn't even tired."

The monk nodded approvingly. "You are beginning to understand. The body has its limitations, but the mind creates the suffering we experience. When you learn to quiet the mind, the body follows naturally. This is the harmony we seek."

Kiran, seated nearby, added with a grin. "He kept up with me by the end. I think he's ready for the lessons here."

The monk laughed softly, his voice carrying both warmth and wisdom. "Each step of the journey prepares you for the next. This monastery is not just a place of learning but of transformation. You will find new challenges here, but also great peace. For now, rest and take in the beauty of this moment. You have earned it."

Harrison leaned back, his eyes drawn once again to the intricate architecture of the monastery. The vaulted ceilings seemed to reach for the heavens, and the walls bore ancient inscriptions that pulsed with quiet energy. Despite its grandeur, there was a simplicity to the space—a sense of purpose that resonated deeply.

"This place... it feels alive," he thought to himself. "As though it holds the wisdom of everyone who has passed through its halls."

The warmth of the fire, the soothing tea, and the presence of his companions filled him with a profound sense of peace. He allowed himself to relax fully, his body and mind finally at ease after the long climb.

He smiled, looking at the monk. "Thank you. For everything. I wouldn't be here without your guidance."

The monk placed a hand on his shoulder. "Your journey is just beginning, my friend. Rest well tonight. Tomorrow, we step further into the depths of self-mastery together."

As the fire crackled softly and the valley below faded into shadow, Harrison felt an unmistakable sense of belonging. This place, these people, this journey—it all felt right, as though it had been waiting for him all along.

For the first time in years, he allowed himself to simply be.

As the fire began to die down, Kiran stood and gestured for Harrison to follow him. He rose, feeling a deep sense of contentment after the warmth of the tea and the peaceful conversation by the hearth. The monk remained by the fire, his serene presence a reassuring anchor.

Kiran led him through a series of quiet, dimly lit hallways. The stone beneath their bare feet was cool but smooth, polished by the countless steps of those who had walked here before. The air was still, carrying the faint scent of incense and mountain herbs.

They arrived at a large dormitory, its simplicity striking. The room was long and open, with neatly arranged beds spaced evenly along the walls. Each bed was identical—a sturdy wooden frame, a thin but comfortable mattress, a folded blanket, and a small shelf above for personal belongings. There were no curtains, no decorations, no indulgences—just clean lines and quiet order.

"This is where we sleep," Kiran said. "Each monk has his own space, and we share the rest. It is simple, but it is all we need."

Harrison placed his bag beside one of the empty beds, running his hand over the smooth wooden frame. At first glance, the room might have seemed austere, but as he stood there, he realised it was exactly what it needed to be. There was a sense of harmony in the uniformity, a quiet dignity in the lack of excess.

"It's so simple," he thought to himself. "No distractions, no clutter—just a place to rest. Why does this feel so perfect?"

Kiran turned to him with a gentle smile. "Sleep well tonight. The air here is pure, the silence deep. You'll find your rest more refreshing than ever before."

Harrison nodded, his heart full. He felt a sudden wave of gratitude for the young monk, for the journey, for everything that had brought him to this place.

He lay down on the bed, the blanket draped lightly over him. The mattress, though firm, felt like a cloud after the day's climb. As he settled, he noticed the subtle sounds of the monastery—the soft footsteps of monks in the hallways, the faint rustle of the wind against the stone walls, the distant hum of a chant carried on the mountain breeze.

For the first time in a long time, he felt no need to check his phone, no urge to scroll through emails or social media. There were no distractions here, no demands on his time or energy. He was fully present, fully at ease.

His body, tired but not strained, sank into the mattress. His mind, calmed by the day's lessons and the monastery's peaceful energy, drifted naturally toward sleep. He thought briefly of the journey ahead, the lessons he would learn, and the person he was becoming.

But those thoughts faded quickly, replaced by a profound sense of contentment. He was here, now, and it was enough.

As the monastery settled into the quiet of night, he slipped into a deep and restful sleep, the kind that felt like it reached into his very soul. It was a sleep filled with peace, untouched by worry or the weight of the outside world. For the first time in years, he felt truly at home.

Chapter Nineteen

A Long Day Begins

The first light of dawn had yet to touch the snow-capped peaks when Harrison awoke, his body refreshed and his mind sharp. He stretched, feeling the residue of yesterday's journey in his muscles—a pleasant ache that spoke of effort and growth. Beside him, Kiran was also stirring, the young monk's slowly and methodically clearing his bed.

"I've never felt this alive in the morning," Harrison thought to himself. "It's as if the air here carries something extra—energy, maybe, or peace."

Kiran noticed his friend's eagerness and smiled. "Come, the day begins early here. We start with asanas to open the body and still the mind, followed by our daily practice. It's a beautiful way to greet the day."

Harrison followed Kiran out of the dormitory and into the crisp pre-dawn air. The monastery was quiet, the stillness punctuated only by the faint rustling of the wind and the occasional call of a bird.

The great hall was vast, its high ceilings and simple stone walls illuminated by the flickering light of oil lamps. Harrison noticed a monk seated at the front, his posture so upright and serene that he seemed carved from stone. It was difficult to determine his age; his face carried both the smoothness of youth and the wisdom of years.

The other monks silently entered, finding their places on the smooth wooden floor. They settled into cross-legged positions, their movements fluid and effortless. Harrison followed their lead, finding a spot near Kiran and lowering himself into a seated position. He closed his eyes, mimicking the stillness around him.

The hall was silent except for the faint crackle of the oil lamps. At first, he found it easy to sit quietly, his body relaxed and his mind calm. But within minutes, his thoughts began to wander.

"Did I pack everything I need for today?" he wondered. "How long will this meditation last? My legs are starting to feel stiff..."

Each time his mind strayed, he brought his focus back to his breath, the gentle rise and fall of his chest. But the wandering thoughts persisted, and now his body was beginning to ache—the familiar tightness in his hips and the dull throb in his lower back.

"This is harder than it looks," he thought. "How do they stay so still?"

Every twenty to thirty seconds, his thoughts would drift, and each time he gently redirected them to his breath or the sensations in his body. It wasn't perfect, but it was progress. After what felt like an eternity, the sound of a singing bowl filled the room, its resonant tone washing over them like a wave.

He opened his eyes, and the monk at the front stood gracefully, his movements unhurried.

Without a word, the monk gestured for the group to stand. What followed was an extraordinary yoga session. The practice began gently, with slow stretches and grounding poses to wake the body. But as the session progressed, the sequences grew more challenging—lunges that burned the thighs, balances that tested focus, and backbends that demanded both strength and surrender.

Harrison struggled at times, his muscles trembling in unfamiliar postures. But he found himself enjoying the challenge, encouraged by the ease and grace of those around him. He focused on his breath, letting it guide him through the discomfort.

"This isn't just about the body," he realised. "It's about the mind, the breath, the connection between them. It's... liberating."

The monk's voice was calm and measured as he guided them through the final postures. And then, at last, came shavasana—the pose of complete rest. Harrison lay on his back, his arms relaxed at his sides, his eyes closed.

As he surrendered to the stillness, a wave of deep relaxation washed over him. The tension in his body melted away, replaced by a profound sense of ease. He felt himself melting into the mat and the mountain.

"This... this is what peace feels like," he thought. "Not forced, not fleeting—just pure, unshakeable stillness."

When the session ended, he sat up slowly, his movements deliberate. His body felt open and alive, his mind clear. He glanced at Kiran, who smiled knowingly.

"This is only the beginning," Kiran said. "Each day, your body and mind will grow stronger, more connected. The real work lies ahead, but you're already on the path."

Harrison nodded, gratitude swelling in his chest. The day had barely begun, but he already felt transformed, ready to embrace whatever came next."This is what I've been searching for," he thought to himself. "Not success, not achievement—just this... peace, this... contentment."

The morning sun streamed through the windows, casting long shadows across the room. The monk at the front of the hall remained seated, his posture effortlessly upright, his gaze calm and steady.

The group, now settled once more, sat in attentive silence as the monk began to speak. His voice was soft but carried a weight that demanded attention.

"What we will do next is the cornerstone of life here at the monastery," the monk began. "It is our daily practice—a sequence of techniques and rituals designed to align the body, mind, and spirit. This practice is not optional. It is not something to fit around the rest of your life—it is the foundation upon which all else must be built."

Harrison listened intently, the gravity of the monk's words sinking in.

"Understand this: all that you seek, all that you desire, is to find peace within yourself. The mind tells you that you need external things—a home, success, recognition—but at the root of every desire is a yearning to feel whole, to be at peace."

He paused, allowing the truth of his words to settle over the room.

"This practice brings that peace. It is why it must come above all else. Whatever happens in your life—no matter the chaos, the joy, the suffering—this practice is your anchor. Without fail, it is performed every day."

Harrison found himself nodding. He had already glimpsed the transformative power of consistent practice in his own life. But there was something more profound in the monk's insistence—a sense that this was not merely a routine but a sacred ritual.

The monk gestured for the group to close their eyes, and the hall fell into stillness. Harrison followed, his breath naturally slowing as the monk began to guide them.

"This practice is taught only within these walls. It is not to be shared, for mastery takes years, and misunderstanding can do more harm than good. Commit to it fully, and it will transform you. But know that it must be learned here, not passed on through words alone."

Harrison felt a sense of reverence settle over him. This was something sacred, something shared by generations of monks who had walked this path before him.

When the practice concluded, the monk rang the singing bowl once more, its resonance filling the room and bringing the group back to the present moment. Harrison opened his eyes, blinking against the soft light that now flooded the hall.

He felt different. There was a stillness inside him, a clarity he couldn't quite describe. Yet, alongside this peace was a vibrant energy—a sense of being fully alive, fully present.

"This isn't just calm," he thought to himself. "It's... something deeper. A strength, maybe. A sense that I can face anything without losing this stillness inside."

The monk looked out over the group, his eyes resting briefly on Harrison.

"This is only the beginning," the monk said. "This practice is not something you master overnight. It is a lifelong journey, and each day brings new depth, new understanding. But already, I can see its effect in you. Carry this with you—not just here in the hall, but in everything you do."

As they rose to leave, Harrison felt a deep gratitude for the experience. Kiran placed a hand on his shoulder, his smile wide and genuine.

"Now you understand why we never miss a day," Kiran said. "This practice is like the sun—it gives life to everything else."

Harrison nodded, feeling fully energised yet calm.

"I've searched for so long," he thought to himself. "For meaning, for peace, for something real. And here it is, in the simplicity of a daily practice. Something I can rely on, something that makes everything else fall into place."

The monks began to file out of the hall, their movements unhurried, their faces serene. Harrison lingered for a moment, taking one last look at the space that already felt so sacred to him. He made a silent promise to himself: I will honour this practice. Every day, no matter what.

With that, he stepped into the light of the new day, feeling ready for whatever lay ahead.

Chapter Twenty

Meeting the Swami

After the morning practice and the peace it brought, Kiran turned to Harrison with a smile.

"It's time for you to meet the head monk, our Swami. He will be your guide throughout your stay. You're very fortunate—his wisdom is unmatched, and his guidance will shape your journey here."

Harrison felt a swell of excitement tempered by a twinge of doubt. Was he worthy of such an honour? Could he rise to the expectations of this great teacher?

Kiran pointed the way and Harrison continued along, ascending the stone steps leading to the monastery's central tower, a structure that seemed to reach toward the heavens. The steps were worn smooth by generations of seekers who had climbed them before. At the top, a large wooden door stood, its surface intricately carved with symbols of peace and enlightenment.

Kiran knocked gently, the sound echoing in the stillness. A voice called from within, and they entered.

By the fire, Harrison saw a figure he immediately recognised. His good friend—the monk who had first set him on this journey—sat serenely, his posture upright, his gaze calm and knowing. Harrison laughed in surprise, his emotions a mix of shock and realisation.

"Of course," he thought to himself. "It all makes sense now. He was the one who started me on this path. And now, he's here to guide me further."

The monk stood and greeted him with a warm smile. "Welcome, my friend. It brings me great joy to see you here."

Harrison felt a surge of respect, admiration, and reverence for the man who had become so much more than a friend. He bowed deeply, his heart full of gratitude.

Kiran excused himself, leaving them alone by the fire.

The two sat in comfortable silence for a moment, the fire crackling softly between them. Finally, the Swami spoke.

"Tell me, what is it you are seeking?"

Harrison didn't hesitate. The answer came to him as clearly as the first rays of the morning sun. "Inner peace."

The Swami smiled, his expression both kind and approving. "Inner peace. It is the foundation upon which all else is built. It is what we all crave, though few realise it. And yes, it is something that grows—not all at once, but with practice, patience, and understanding."

Harrison felt the weight of those words, their simplicity carrying a profound truth.

"I would like you to stay here with us for forty days," the Swami continued. "During this time, your focus will be on two things. First, developing focus and concentration. Your daily practice will be your greatest teacher in this. It must become your highest priority. Second, understanding how to be at peace. This requires a concise understanding of the mind and body. You have already been introduced to these concepts, but over the next forty days, we will deepen this knowledge until it becomes your own knowing."

Harrison nodded, feeling a sense of purpose settle over him.

"My hope is that you will take what you learn here and share it with the West," the Swami added. "The world is in need of this wisdom, and your voice can reach new people."

The Swami reached beside him and handed Harrison three simple robes, the soft fabric folded neatly.

"Here are your robes," the Swami said. "For the next forty days, I encourage you to let go of anything you don't truly need. The more you release, the more freedom you will find."

Harrison held the robes, their simplicity a stark contrast to the life he had left behind. He realised how much lighter he already felt, having loosened his grip on possessions and identity during the journey.

"What do you think you will need for the next forty days?" the Swami asked.

Harrison smiled, the answer coming easily. "My notepad and a pen, my robes, food, water, soap... and lots of guidance."

The Swami chuckled, his eyes twinkling. "Good. Simplicity is not deprivation—it brings much clarity. And clarity brings peace."

The Swami explained the structure of Harrison's days, each one carefully designed to balance discipline and understanding.

"Padmasanesh, the monk from the morning practice, will guide you in asanas and your daily practice. These sessions will help you develop focus, clear your mind, and strengthen your body. Kiran will guide you through the daily chores. He has a natural joyfulness and a mastery of the beginner's mind. Though he is young, there is much you can learn from him."

"Your days will also include two meals—breakfast and dinner—and an evening practice to close the day. This is a simple life, but it is rich with purpose. Each moment here is an opportunity to grow."

Harrison absorbed every word, the weight of the forty-day commitment settling into him. But instead of fear or hesitation, he felt excitement—a chance to delve deeper into himself, to uncover the peace he had been seeking for so long.

Chapter Twenty One

The Breakfast Practice

Harrison and the Swami descended the stone steps together, the morning sunlight streaming through the high windows of the monastery. The air was crisp, carrying the faint aroma of spices and freshly cooked food. They walked in comfortable silence, the Swami's calm presence a grounding force for Harrison.

As they entered the dining hall, he was impressed by its simplicity. Long wooden tables stretched the length of the room, flanked by benches. Monks moved quietly, their robes rustling softly as they gathered their meals. There was no chatter, no rush, just an atmosphere of peaceful purpose.

Kiran approached with a warm smile and gestured for Harrison to follow him to the serving area.

Breakfast consisted of three simple dishes: a warm porridge, freshly baked flatbread, and a small bowl of fruit. Each item was prepared with care, their vibrant colours and aromas speaking of freshness and simplicity. The monks serving the food handed each portion to Harrison with gentle smiles, their kindness and joy of giving unmistakable.

"Even in the act of serving, there's a sense of reverence," Harrison thought to himself. "It's as if every moment here is imbued with meaning."

Harrison carried his tray back to the table where the Swami and Kiran were already seated. He noticed how they sat with straight backs, their movements deliberate. He mirrored their posture, his senses heightened by the calm energy of the room.

The hall was silent as the monks began their meal. Harrison followed their lead, picking up his spoon and pausing to observe the food before him. He looked closely at the oats, noting their golden hue, the steam rising gently. He brought the food to his nose and inhaled, the earthy aroma grounding him in the moment.

Taking his first mouthful, he chewed slowly, savouring the textures and flavours. The warmth of the porridge spread through him, and he noticed how much more satisfying the experience was when he gave it his full attention. Each mouthful was deliberate—he didn't reach for the next bite until he had fully tasted and appreciated the one before.

The flatbread was soft and fragrant, its simple flavour a perfect complement to the oats. The fruit was sweet, juicy, and bursting with freshness. After paying so much attention to the subtle flavours of the porridge, the fruit felt like such a treat.

As he ate, he noticed that the other monks were completely absorbed in their meals. No one rushed, no one spoke. The silence wasn't awkward; it was intentional, a shared practice of mindfulness.

"Even eating is a practice here," he thought. "A training in appreciation, focus, and beginner's mind."

He looked at Kiran, who smiled warmly before returning to his meal. The young monk's movements were graceful, his presence serene. Harrison marvelled at how even something as ordinary as breakfast could be transformed into a profound experience.

As they finished, Harrison turned to the Swami, speaking softly so as not to disturb the others.

"This way of eating... it's so simple but incredible. I've never been so aware of each bite. There is so much more depth to the flavour when you pay attention."

The Swami nodded, his expression kind. "Eating, like every other act, is an opportunity to train the mind. When we focus fully on what we are doing, whether it's eating, walking, or even breathing, we cultivate awareness. We train ourselves to be present. And when we are present, we appreciate life more fully."

Harrison felt the truth of those words. He thought back to his life before the monastery, how meals had been rushed, eaten while distracted by work or scrolling through his phone. He realised how much he had missed—how much joy had slipped by unnoticed.

"If I can bring this level of awareness to everything I do," he thought to himself, "life will feel richer, more vibrant, and I can find happiness in the smallest of things."

As they rose to clear their trays, Harrison couldn't help but smile. He had always thought of training as specific physical or mental exercises for the body or learning for the mind. But now he realised this was a completely different kind of training, far more practical for real life.

"Every task, no matter how small, can be a practice," he reflected. "A way to hone my mind, to deepen my appreciation for life. It's all about how I approach it."

The three of them walked out into the courtyard, the morning sun now bright against the snowy peaks. Harrison felt a renewed sense of purpose, ready for the lessons that lay ahead. The simplicity of the meal had left him not only nourished but energised, his mind and body aligned for the day's practice.

The Swami placed a hand on his shoulder as they paused at the edge of the courtyard.

"Peace isn't found in grand moments," he said, "but in the small, consistent practices that shape our lives. With this method, we can slowly become skilful at living our day-to-day life in appreciation."

Harrison nodded, the words resonating deeply. With each step, each breath, he was learning to live fully.

Chapter Twenty Two

Washing the Dishes

The morning sun bathed the courtyard in golden light as Harrison and Kiran lingered after breakfast. Feeling energised from the meal and the morning practice, he turned to Kiran with curiosity.

"What will we do today?"

Kiran grinned, his youthful enthusiasm infectious. "Today, we work. Over the next forty days, we'll take on most of the tasks needed to run the monastery. This is how we live—each task is part of our practice. We'll start simple: washing up from breakfast."

Harrison nodded, eager to contribute and ready to prove his worth.

They returned to the dining hall, where plates, bowls, and cups were stacked neatly at the tables. Harrison quickly set to work, stacking a full tray of dishes with precision and efficiency. He glanced over at Kiran, who was moving at a much slower pace, carefully collecting each plate one by one.

"I've got this. I can be useful here," Harrison thought to himself.

Feeling a surge of satisfaction, he carried the tray to the kitchen, eager to fill another. He was already imagining how much faster he could finish the job, how productive he could be.

In the kitchen, two large basins were set up. One filled with soapy water and the other with clean water for rinsing. Harrison and Kiran were joined by another monk, an older man whose serene movements exuded calm. The older monk took up the task of rinsing the plates, passing them to Harrison to dry.

Harrison kept pace easily, his movements brisk and efficient. But soon, he found himself waiting for the others to pass him more plates.

"This is going to take forever at this rate," he thought to himself. "Why are we moving so slowly?"

Unable to hold back, he spoke up. "I could take over cleaning. We'd be done in half the time."

Kiran smiled, his expression a blend of amusement and patience. "There's no rush. The goal isn't to finish washing the dishes. The goal is to enjoy washing each dish."

Harrison blinked, confused. "Enjoy washing each dish?" This was so different to how he did things, so simple but also very confronting.

Kiran gestured to the older monk, whose every movement seemed deliberate, almost meditative. The monk dipped each dish into the soapy water, scrubbing gently, then passed it to the rinse basin with care. His face bore a quiet smile, as though he were savouring the task.

"Watch him," Kiran said. "Each movement is intentional, each action complete in itself. There's no rush, no stress, just presence. When you rush, you're focused on the end, not the task. But life is happening in the task."

Though the concept seemed foreign, Harrison decided to give it a try. He picked up a wet plate, drying it slowly. At first, his mind rebelled.

"This is too slow," he thought to himself. "There's so much more to do. We'll never finish like this."

But as he forced himself to slow down, he noticed something shift. The sensation of the warm plate in his hands, the texture of the towel, the gentle sound of the dishes clinking together—all of it became more vivid. He began to observe his own thoughts: the need to rush, the desire to compete, the urge to achieve.

"Why am I always in such a hurry?" he wondered. "What am I rushing toward?"

With each dish, he felt himself settle further into the process. Drying the plates became less of a task and more of an experience. He no longer counted how many were left or worried about how long it would take. He simply dried one plate, then another, then another.

An hour later, the last plate was placed on the drying rack. He set down his towel, feeling a surprising sense of accomplishment—not because the job was done, but because of how he had done it.

Kiran led him outside, where they sat on a stone bench overlooking the snow-dusted mountains. The air was crisp, and the sunlight warmed their faces.

"How do you feel?" Kiran asked.

Harrison thought for a moment, then smiled. "Calm. Focused. I didn't think I could enjoy washing dishes. It's so different from how I've always done things."

Kiran nodded. "When we rush, we're disconnected—from the task, from the moment, even from ourselves. When we slow down, we reconnect. Every task can be an enjoyable practice if we approach it with the right mindset."

Harrison gazed out at the mountains, the weight of Kiran's words sinking in.

"Every moment, every task, every breath," he thought to himself. "It's all an opportunity to practice, to live fully. Even washing dishes can be meaningful if I let it be."

As the wind carried the scent of snow and incense, he felt a growing sense of peace. The simplicity of each moment was enough.

Chapter Twenty Three

Clearing the Steps

After their morning tasks in the kitchen, Kiran led Harrison to the wide stone staircase that descended from the monastery's entrance. The snow from the previous night had blanketed the steps in a thick, icy layer, rendering them almost invisible. Clearing the steps wasn't just essential for the safety of the monks and visitors. It was also a practice in itself, an exercise in patience, focus, and presence.

Kiran handed Harrison a simple wooden shovel and smiled warmly.

"Today, we clear the steps," Kiran said. "Slowly, with care. Bring a beginner's mind to each moment. Aim to be conscious of each movement and learn to appreciate what's there in each moment. Consciously choose to not create and also let go of any internal resistance."

Harrison nodded, but a pang of reluctance flickered within him. The task seemed endless, the staircase stretching far below them like an insurmountable challenge. The cold air bit at his cheeks, and the shovel felt heavy in his hands.

They began at the top. Kiran moved with deliberate grace, demonstrating how to gently scoop and push the snow aside without rushing. Each movement seemed effortless and precise, his focus unwavering. Harrison mimicked his movements, and for the first few minutes, he was able to apply a beginner's mind well. Each motion felt fresh—new even. He noticed the texture of the snow as it crunched under the shovel, the sharp chill of the air filling his lungs, the soft glimmer of sunlight on the frozen crystals.

For a while, he felt deeply present—appreciating not just the task but everything around him. His companion Kiran, the view stretching out across the valley below, the way the clouds hugged the peaks of distant mountains.

But after about ten minutes, Harrison's focus began to slip. His mind filled with thoughts: How long will this take? Will we even finish by sunset? It's so cold. My hands are freezing.

Each time he noticed his thoughts spiralling, he reminded himself of Kiran's words—aim to be conscious of each movement and learn to appreciate what's there in each moment. He brought his attention back to the shovel, to the motion of clearing one step at a time.

As the minutes turned into hours, something shifted. He let go—there was nothing to do, nowhere to be, no one to please. The task became enjoyable, peaceful, effortless. The scrape of the shovel against stone, the soft thud of snow landing on the growing piles beside the steps, the steady inhale and exhale of his breath.

His mind still wandered frequently, but each time he noticed this, he was able to bring his mind back to the task, reminding himself to focus on a beginner's mind and observing each movement. Each time he applied beginner's mind, he felt a fresh appreciation for that moment. He was slowly realising no two shovels of snow were alike. Each was new, and as this understanding grew, so did his appreciation.

"It's like washing the dishes," he thought to himself. "There's no rush, no goal except to be here, doing this with my good friend."

The sun climbed higher in the sky, its warmth cutting through the chill. Lunchtime came and went, but Harrison observed he didn't feel hungry. He was sustained by the simplicity of the work, by the deep, almost meditative rhythm of their efforts.

Beside him, Kiran worked steadily, smiling softly with each movement. There was no urgency in his actions, just presence. A calm acceptance of the task. Harrison felt a quiet joy radiating from Kiran, and it was infectious.

As the sun dipped lower on the horizon, casting a golden glow across the snowy peaks, they cleared the final step. The staircase now stood clean and safe, its smooth stone glistening faintly in the fading light.

Harrison straightened slowly, leaning his shovel against the wall. His back ached slightly, his arms felt heavy, but there was a deep sense of satisfaction in his chest. A fullness he hadn't felt in a long time.

"We did that," he thought. "Step by step, without rushing, without forcing. It feels... good. Not just the result, but the process itself was good."

Kiran clapped him on the back, his grin wide and genuine. "Beautiful work, Harrison. Come, let's climb the steps and enjoy them properly."

Harrison laughed, though his legs felt heavy as they ascended. But each step carried a new weight, not just from the day's labour but from the appreciation that had grown within him.

With every step upward, he felt connected to the work they had done, to the simplicity of the moment, and to the quiet joy that came from embracing the process rather than fixating on the end result.

At the top of the staircase, they paused to catch their breath. The monastery lay behind them, smoke curling gently from the chimney, and the vast expanse of the mountains stretched out before them.

Harrison felt something profound settle inside him. A clarity, a peace, and a quiet pride in the simple act of showing up fully for each moment.

"It was never about clearing the steps," he realised. "It was about clearing my mind. Breaking the habits, the cycles of thoughts and movements that I've built up over a lifetime."

With that thought, they turned and walked back toward the monastery, their steps slow and deliberate, their hearts light with contentment.

Chapter Twenty Four

A Monks Rest

At the top of the steps, Harrison sighed, his body longing for rest. "I think I need to lie down. Or at least have some time to myself."

Kiran shook his head, his eyes twinkling with a knowing light. "I have something better. A meditation. Trust me—it's exactly what you need."

Though meditation felt like the last thing he wanted, Harrison trusted Kiran's judgement. Together, they made their way to the great hall, where the other monks were already gathering. The room was bathed in the soft glow of lanterns, their light flickering gently against the stone walls. The air was thick with the warm, earthy scent of incense, wrapping around them like a soft blanket.

Harrison took his place, sitting cross-legged with the others, his body heavy and his mind scattered.

The session began with Padmasanesh inviting them to lie down. Harrison sank gratefully onto his back, his body melting into the floor as the cold and tension in his muscles began to ease. Padmasanesh's calm, steady voice guided them through a series of slow, deliberate movements, each one designed to release tension and restore energy.

To Harrison's surprise, his body responded quickly. The dull aches faded, his muscles softened, and a sense of lightness returned. It was as though each stretch wrung out a knot of tension, leaving behind space and ease. As they transitioned into a calming breathing practice, Harrison found his focus sharpening. His breath became an anchor for his wandering mind, gently pulling his awareness back to the present moment.

Finally, they moved into seated meditation. At first, Harrison struggled—his mind darted from one thought to another, and his head nodded forward as sleep tried to pull him under. Each time he jerked awake, he brought his focus back to the faint sensation of breath at the tip of his nose, just as Padmasanesh had instructed.

As the minutes stretched on, something began to shift. The grip of his wandering thoughts loosened, and stillness began to take root. By the end of the session, his mind was quieter, his energy restored. He opened his eyes to find Padmasanesh standing nearby, smiling gently.

Padmasanesh sat down beside him, his posture so still, alert but also effortless.

"How was the practice?" Padmasanesh asked.

"I struggled a lot at the start," Harrison replied. "My body was tired, and my mind was all over the place. But as we went on, I relaxed, and by the end, I felt... focused. Energised, even."

Padmasanesh nodded, his smile steady. "This is the nature of the practice. At first, the body resists, the mind resists. But with patience and persistence, both begin to settle."

Harrison hesitated, his gaze dropping to his hands before meeting the monk's eyes again.

"I still get distracted so easily—by thoughts, by my body. It feels like I'll never be able to focus fully."

Padmasanesh's expression was kind, his voice gentle but firm. "Distraction is natural, especially in the beginning. The body will quiet down over time. This is why we practise asanas, to still the body so we can sit with ease. The mind, too, will slow, but it requires a point of focus. This is where your breath becomes your anchor."

He gestured lightly toward Harrison's nose. "Focus on the sensations here, at the tip of your nose, as you breathe. Each time your mind wanders, gently bring it back. Don't fight the distractions—simply notice them and return to your focus. Bit by bit, you will develop the skill of concentration. It is like training a muscle."

Harrison nodded, the monk's words resonating deeply within him. "It's not about perfection," he thought. "It's about practice. Each time I bring my focus back, I'm strengthening that skill. This isn't about forcing the mind to be still—it's about guiding it, gently, with patience."

As the session concluded, Harrison felt a quiet satisfaction settle over him. The day's labour, the meditation, the lessons—they had all woven together into something meaningful, something he could feel growing within him but couldn't yet fully articulate.

As he entered the dining hall for dinner, the room glowed warmly with the light of lanterns. The air was alive with the quiet hum of purposeful movements as monks moved gracefully between tables, carrying trays of steaming dishes. Tonight's meal was more elaborate than breakfast. There were five beautifully prepared vegetarian dishes, each simple yet bursting with flavour and care. The aroma of spices, roasted vegetables, and fresh herbs hung heavy in the air, making Harrison's mouth water.

He joined Kiran and a few monks at their table. As the meal began, Harrison committed himself to the practice he was learning—mindful eating.

He picked up his spoon, pausing to observe the lentil curry before him. Its rich scent rose warmly, and as he took his first bite, the flavours bloomed on his tongue. A perfect harmony of warmth and spice. It took every ounce of discipline not to immediately rush into the next mouthful.

"It's so good, and I'm so hungry," he thought. "But this is practice, just like everything else. Each bite is an opportunity to learn."

He glanced at the other monks around him. Each was immersed in their own meals, their movements unhurried, their focus complete. They savoured each bite as though it were their first, their last, their only.

After dinner, the monks were given thirty minutes of free time. Harrison stepped outside, feeling the weight of the day settle over him. Not an exhaustion, but a deep, satisfying tiredness. It was the feeling of having been fully present, fully alive.

He sat down on the monastery's stone steps, gazing out into the cool night. The air carried the faint scent of incense and snow, and above him, the sky stretched infinitely, scattered with innumerable bright stars. The mountains framed the horizon like silent guardians, their peaks kissed by the faint glow of moonlight.

"What a day," he thought to himself. "It feels like I've lived a lifetime in these hours, but I'm not drained. It's as if this way of life fuels me rather than exhausts me. I never knew I had the capacity to do so much."

He closed his eyes and let the stillness wash over him. There was no rush, no noise, no sense of urgency, just a quiet peace in which he could simply be.

When the bell tolled softly in the distance, signalling the evening gathering, he rose and made his way to the great hall.

Chapter Twenty Five

The Six Pillars of Understanding

The hall was already filled with monks, each seated cross-legged on their mats in perfect stillness. The flickering lanterns cast gentle shadows on the stone walls, and the soothing scent of incense lingered in the cool mountain air. At the front of the hall sat the Swami, his eyes closed, his posture straight and still, like an ancient tree rooted deeply in the earth.

The room fell into an unforced silence as the remaining monks settled into their seats. The quiet wasn't heavy or awkward; it was natural, a collective presence shared effortlessly by everyone in the room.

Harrison followed suit, sitting upright and closing his eyes. He let his breath slow, his shoulders soften, and his mind ease into the shared stillness of the space.

After several minutes, the Swami slowly opened his eyes, scanning the room with a warm, knowing smile.

"Tonight, we will discuss the six pillars of our understanding," he began. "These form the foundation of our practice and guide us toward inner peace.

They are:

Desires

- Internal Experience
- Enjoyment—Appreciation—Beginner's Mind
- Seek What's Real—Establish What We Are Not
- Non-Suffering
- And finally, the most important pillar, which I will discuss individually with each of you at the end of your forty days here."

The weight of those words hung gently in the air. Harrison leaned forward slightly, anticipation sparking within him.

The Swami turned and gestured to a younger monk seated nearby. "Please, share your insights on each of these pillars."

The young monk stood, bowing respectfully to the Swami and the assembly before he began to speak.

"Desires," the monk began, "are the root of our suffering. They pull us away from the present, convincing us that happiness lies somewhere in the future—in acquiring, achieving, or controlling something. But true happiness is found in letting go of desires and being fully at peace with what is, right now."

Harrison absorbed the words, feeling their truth resonate deeply.

"Internal Experience," the monk continued, his voice steady and clear. "Our entire experience of life happens within us. Nothing external—no object, no person, no event can directly make us feel good or bad. Only our interpretation creates our internal experience. When we realise this, we regain control over how we respond to life. The choice is always within us."

"Seek what's real—Establish what we are not," the monk continued. "To find peace, we must simplify life and clarify for ourselves what is real and what is not. Identity is a construct of the mind, built from our possessions, roles, relationships, and beliefs. But none of these truly define who we are. When we recognise something as false like a thought, an expectation, an identity—we must learn to reject it. What remains is closer to our true self."

Harrison felt a shift within him. He had begun this journey of unlearning, and each layer he shed felt like a step towards freedom.

"Beginner's mind—Enjoyment, appreciation," the monk's voice carried on with gentle authority. "When we approach each moment with a beginner's mind, we strip away expectations and see reality as it is—fresh, alive, and full of wonder. Each moment becomes an opportunity for joy, for appreciation. But like all the other pillars, this is a skill. It grows through practice, through attention, and through humility."

The idea of beginner's mind felt like a golden key—a way to unlock peace in every corner of life.

"Non-Suffering," the monk concluded. "Pain is inevitable; it is part of life. But suffering is a choice, a reaction to resisting what is. Suffering arises when we wish reality were different from what it is. When we let go of that resistance and accept each moment fully, we release ourselves from suffering."

Harrison closed his eyes briefly, letting these words settle in. Pain is real, but suffering is optional. The simplicity and power of this truth struck him deeply. Imagine a life free from suffering.

The young monk bowed and returned to his seat, and the Swami once again addressed the room.

"These pillars are not merely ideas—they are practices. They must become part of how you live, how you think, how you respond. Over the next forty days, you will explore them deeply, not just with your mind, but with your entire being. Allow them to shape you, to transform you, to guide you."

The room was silent again, but now it was a silence rich with thought, reflection, and resolve.

Harrison sat with his eyes closed, the words of the six pillars turning over in his mind like precious stones. They felt both vast and deeply personal, guiding principles that could shape not just the next forty days, but the rest of his life.

As the monks began to quietly file out of the hall, Harrison lingered for a moment. The weight of the day settled over him, not a burden, but a fullness, a sense of meaningful effort and quiet clarity.

As he walked back to the dormitory, the stars overhead seemed brighter, the air felt cleaner, and each step carried a new lightness.

"If this is what one day here feels like," he thought to himself, "I can only imagine what the next forty will bring."

With that thought lingering warmly in his mind, Harrison lay down on his simple bed, closed his eyes, and slipped into a deep, restful sleep.

Chapter Twenty Six

A Week of Practice

The days at the monastery unfolded with a quiet, steady rhythm. Each morning, Harrison awoke before the sun, energised by the cool mountain air and the clarity that his daily practice brought. He had quickly adjusted to the pace of life here—it was simple, purposeful, and deeply fulfilling.

Every morning began in the great hall with asanas and the monastery's sacred daily practice. Harrison noticed that with each passing day, his body grew more flexible, his breath steadier, and his mind calmer. Though he still struggled with occasional distractions, his focus was improving, and he began to experience moments of deep stillness that felt profoundly transformative.

Throughout the week, Harrison worked alongside Kiran and the other monks on tasks essential to the monastery's upkeep. Each task, no matter how small, was treated with great care and as an opportunity to practise mindfulness and focus.

Sweeping the Courtyard: The sound of the broom against the stone, the feel of the wooden handle in his hands. It all became part of his meditation. He noticed how his mind would wander to the past or future, and each time, he gently brought it back to the present.

Tending the Garden: Planting and watering the herbs and vegetables taught him patience. He observed how each action contributed to the growth of the plants, just as each moment of focus contributed to his own growth. It also brought an even greater appreciation to his meals.

Helping in the Kitchen: Even preparing food became a source of joy. The aroma of spices, the vibrant colours of fresh ingredients. It all felt alive in a way he hadn't noticed before.

But the true joy came from giving. Kiran taught him to pour his love into each dish by focusing on the monks and the Swami, preparing each meal as an act of service and gratitude.

Through these activities, Harrison began to see the wisdom in Kiran's words: "Every task is a practice. As we practice, we become more skilful and our experience of life will deepen."

The Growth of Focus and Concentration

Bit by bit, Harrison noticed subtle but powerful changes within himself. His ability to stay present grew stronger with each passing day. Tasks that once felt tedious or repetitive now brought a sense of calm and purpose. He was beginning to understand that focus and concentration weren't just skills, they were states of being.

One afternoon, as he cleared snow from a narrow path leading to the meditation hall, he realised that an hour had passed without his mind drifting once. Instead of feeling tired, he felt energised and alive.

"This is what they mean by peace," he thought to himself. "It can't be attained by something external—it's something you cultivate within yourself."

Throughout the week, he also learned more about the monastery and its teachings. Conversations with Kiran, the Swami, and the other monks offered him new insights into himself and the world around him.

From Kiran: The young monk's joy and beginner's mind continued to inspire Harrison. One day, as they worked together to clean the temple steps, Kiran said, "We are all students, no matter how old or wise we become. The moment we think we've mastered something is the moment we stop learning."

From the Swami: During evening gatherings, the Swami shared profound teachings about the nature of the mind, the power of stillness, and the importance of consistency. "A single day of practice will not transform you," he said one evening, "but a lifetime of practice will shape you into something extraordinary."

From the Monks: Each monk brought a unique perspective to Harrison's journey, whether through their words or their silent example. Watching them move through their days with grace and ease, Harrison began to see what it meant to live joyfully in peace.

By the end of the week, he felt a profound sense of gratitude for the life he was living. Though the days were physically demanding and required intense focus, he found them deeply rewarding. He no longer felt the constant pull of distractions or the need to rush through tasks. Instead, he embraced each moment fully, knowing that it was part of a greater whole.

One evening, as he sat on the monastery steps watching the sun dip below the mountains, he reflected on how far he had come in just a few days.

"This life feels so simple," he thought to himself, "yet it's more meaningful than anything I've ever experienced. It's not about achieving or accumulating—it's about being present, being connected, and finding peace within myself."

The week had been a quiet revelation, a glimpse of what life could be when lived with awareness. As Harrison prepared for the days ahead, he felt ready to dive even deeper into this journey of transformation.

Chapter Twenty Seven

The Silent Challenge

That evening, the monks gathered in the great hall as usual. The air was still, the flickering lanterns casting warm light on the serene faces around the room. The Swami sat at the front, his presence commanding yet calm.

After a brief moment of silence, he began to speak.

"Tomorrow, we begin a practice of silence that will last for four days," he said. "During this time, you must not speak or communicate in any way. No gestures, no writing, no physical signals. Each of you will be assigned a task that allows you to work independently, so there will be no need for interaction."

The room bristled with excitement at this new challenge, with the monks quietly sharing a final smile with each other.

Harrison felt a mix of emotions. Excitement at the challenge and trepidation at its difficulty. He had grown used to the simplicity of life at the monastery, but the idea of complete silence was daunting.

"No talking, no gesturing, no sharing a smile or nod?" he thought to himself. "This is going to be a real test."

The Swami continued. "The purpose of this practice is to deepen your awareness. Without the distraction of communication, you will have the chance to observe your thoughts, your habits, and your inner world more clearly. The first day will be the most challenging. You will work through a lot of karma, breaking many long-held habits. Let it be an opportunity for growth and transformation."

After the meeting, the monks were assigned their tasks for the week. Harrison's task was to bring drinking water in from the lake. A job he had done with Kiran the previous week. He remembered the cool, clear water and the rhythmic process of carrying the buckets back to the monastery.

"At least I know how to do it," he thought. "This task feels manageable, even with the silence."

From that moment on, the rule of silence began. There was no more speaking, no more nodding in agreement, no more quiet laughter at Kiran's jokes. The monks dispersed to their quarters in stillness, gently walking with even more care than normal.

As Harrison lay down on his simple bed, he reflected on the challenge ahead.

"At least the first eight hours will be easy—I'll be asleep!"

He drifted off with a mix of anticipation and unease, the silence already settling over the monastery like a gentle but powerful wave.

The First Morning

Harrison woke early, as usual, the cold mountain air sharp and invigorating. The monastery was silent, except for the soft rustling of robes and the occasional creak of wooden floorboards. Without the usual morning chatter or Kiran's cheerful smile, the atmosphere felt different. It felt like a great step up in taking responsibility for his own internal experience.

He made his way to the great hall for morning practice. The monks moved with their usual grace, their footsteps soft and deliberate. The absence of sound heightened his awareness of every detail: the whisper of robes, the rhythmic breathing during asanas, the distant chirping of birds outside.

At first, Harrison struggled to keep his mind from wandering. He regularly felt compelled to share his experience and thoughts with others; he realised he was constantly seeking validation.

"I didn't realise how much I rely on talking and connecting with others to validate my actions, my thoughts," he reflected. "This silence leaves me alone with my mind."

Fetching Water

After a breakfast eaten in complete silence, with even greater mindfulness than usual, Harrison set out for the lake. The path wound down through the forest, the sound of his footsteps crunching on the snow his only companion in the serene stillness of the morning.

Reaching the lake, he picked up the two wooden buckets left by the previous day's worker. The water was icy cold, and as he dipped the first bucket into the lake, he felt a surge of gratitude for its clarity and abundance.

Carrying the full buckets back to the monastery was no small feat. The weight tested his balance, and the cold bit at his hands. Without Kiran's usual encouragement, he found himself relying on his own inner resolve.

"This isn't just about strength," he thought to himself. "It's about non-suffering, about finding ease in the task."

He began to settle into a steady pace, his breath matching his movements. By the time he returned to the monastery and set the buckets down, he felt a deep sense of accomplishment. When he thought of the monks drinking this water, he felt so much appreciation. This task felt like such an honour, such a wonderful thing to do. Each movement could become an act of love and care, and each time he connected with this, he felt so much joy.

Observations in Silence

Throughout the day, the silence began to reveal things Harrison hadn't noticed before. Without the distractions of conversation, he became acutely aware of his own habits and thoughts.

The urge to communicate: On several occasions, he found himself wanting to smile at a fellow monk or nod in gratitude when someone held a door for him. Each time, he caught himself and let the urge pass, realising how automatic these gestures had become.

Heightened awareness: The lack of interaction brought a new clarity to his surroundings. He noticed the way the light filtered through the trees, the intricate patterns of frost on the windows, the soft hum of life all around him.

Inner restlessness: He also faced moments of frustration. Without the outlet of speech, he really became aware of the small negative noises and things he would often say. Like groans, sighs or comments. These things just made him and others feel bad, there was no benefit. Without engaging in these, they dispersed so quickly. Not only didn't he need them, they actually made his experience of life worse.

Chapter Twenty Eight

Reflection at Day's End

As the sun dipped below the mountains, he sat on the monastery steps, the cold stone beneath him grounding him in the moment. The silence felt less oppressive now, more like a blanket wrapping around him, inviting him to look inward.

The first day of silence had been a challenge, but he reflected on how freeing it had also been. Without the constant pressure to engage, to make others like him, or to seek approval, he felt lighter. He realised how much of his energy had been consumed by these unconscious habits, and how unnecessary they seemed in the stillness of silence.

"It's like I am on holiday from my identity," he thought to himself. "No expectations, no performances—just being."

"It's teaching me so much. I'm starting to see how much noise I create. Not just with my words, but in my mind. Without that noise, there's so much space. Space to think, to feel, to be."

He watched as the stars emerged one by one, their light sharp and brilliant in the clear mountain sky. The first day of silence had been challenging, but it had also been such a gift, a chance to listen, not just with his ears, but with his heart. As he prepared for the days ahead, he felt a quiet determination to embrace the practice fully.

The Swami's Lesson

That evening in the great hall, the monks gathered again. The Swami sat at the front, his eyes warm as he observed the group. The silence in the room was palpable, yet it carried no awkwardness, only calm anticipation.

When he spoke, his voice was soft but clear.

"You have done well today. Silence can be challenging, but it also reveals much about ourselves. I trust you are beginning to see this."

Harrison nodded internally, his mind flashing back to moments throughout the day when he had felt both the struggle and the freedom of silence.

"Tomorrow, we will deepen the practice," the Swami continued. "Today, you refrained from communicating with others. But many of you, I suspect, have continued to talk... to yourselves."

Harrison's eyes widened. He had indeed been narrating his day in his mind, analysing tasks, replaying conversations, and planning the future. The realisation hit him: even in silence, the chatter in his head hadn't stopped.

"When you speak to yourself, you are still engaging in a form of communication, one that pulls you away from the present moment," the Swami explained. "For the second day of silence, I ask you to let go of this inner dialogue. Do not speak to yourself. Simply observe."

As Harrison walked back to his room, the Swami's words echoed in his mind. He thought about how much time he spent talking to himself—narrating his experiences, judging his actions, imagining conversations. It was a constant stream of thought, and it felt almost impossible to turn off.

"How do I stop talking to myself? Isn't that just... thinking?" he wondered, then observed he was talking now and let this question go.

But as he lay in bed, he began to understand. He was talking a lot in his head, and each time he spoke to himself, he could choose not to respond, not to engage with the thoughts, to let them pass without clinging to them or responding. It was about stepping back and observing further. Each time he watched and didn't respond, the thought quickly disappeared.

Harrison drifted off to sleep with a sense of anticipation. The first day had felt like a break from the pressures of external identity. Now, the second day would challenge him to step even further away from the roles and stories he carried in his own mind.

The silence was not just about refraining from speech; it was about stepping into a deeper kind of freedom. Though he knew it would be difficult, he also knew it was a gift.

Chapter Twenty Nine

Observing Judging

The second day of silence had been profound for Harrison. Though challenging, it brought a clarity he hadn't experienced before. He became acutely aware of how often he spoke to himself. There was an endless inner monologue that narrated, planned, and analysed every moment of his life. But as he observed these thoughts without engaging in them, they began to lose their power. By the end of the day, his mind had quieted considerably.

That evening, as he entered the great hall, the silence felt deeper and more tangible. The Swami's calm gaze swept over the monks before he began to speak.

"Well done. You have begun to see the chatter of the mind for what it is, and with that awareness comes freedom. Now, let us turn our attention to another aspect of the mind's activity: Judging."

Harrison leaned forward slightly, curious.

"The mind is constantly judging—others, situations, even yourself. It does this to affirm your identity. Each time you judge someone, you're essentially saying, 'I am better at this thing.' This judgement carries a reward, you feel good, and this is why the mind repeats it so frequently."

Harrison's eyes widened as the Swami continued.

"Judging creates separation; it feeds the illusion that we are different, better, worse and ultimately separate from others. It reinforces the false self. Over the next day, I encourage you to observe this judging. Don't fight it, and don't try to stop it. Simply notice it, label it as judging, and let it pass."

Judgement Unveiled

As Harrison left the hall that evening, the lesson was fresh in his mind. He walked slowly, savouring the peace he felt, the stillness that came from a day of reduced inner chatter. He noticed some monks rising and moving more quickly than he was and felt a flicker of judgement arise.

"They should be slow like me. They don't understand the peace, I do," he thought to himself.

The realisation hit him like a bolt of lightning: this was exactly what the Swami had described. His mind was judging others to affirm his own sense of superiority.

"Judging. That's judging," he noted silently.

He labelled it, let it be, and continued walking. The judgement dissipated as quickly as it had arisen.

As Harrison tidied his mat and prepared to leave the hall, the habit of judgement became glaringly apparent again. He noticed some mats left crooked and felt another judgement surface.

"Those mats aren't straight. But I'll put mine straight," he caught himself. "Wow, this is me judging, saying I'm better at this."

Again, he caught the thought, labelled it as judging, and let it pass. The more he paid attention, the more he realised how pervasive the habit was.

A monk held the door open for him, meeting his eyes with a warm, unspoken acknowledgment. Harrison felt an immediate flicker of judgement. "He's breaking the silence, communicating. I am judging again, saying I am better." He observed the thought, labelled it, and let it go.

The process was eye-opening. Harrison hadn't realised how much of his mental energy was spent on judging others, often for trivial things, just to affirm his own sense of self-worth.

The next day, he made a conscious effort to continue observing his judgements. At first, they arose frequently, almost constantly when around others. While he fetched water, while he ate, even while he sat in meditation. Each time, he labelled the thought as judging and let it pass without engaging.

Gradually, he noticed a shift. The frequency of judgements began to decrease, and their pull on him weakened. By the end of the day, he felt lighter, as though a burden he hadn't even realised he was carrying had been lifted.

"It's amazing," he reflected. "Just by observing, by not engaging, these habits lose their momentum. The mind slows, and peace grows."

"Judging creates separation," he thought. "But as I let it go, connection and peace grows."

Chapter Thirty

The Art of Skilful Speech

The great hall was alive with an unusual energy that night. Though the silence remained unbroken, Harrison could sense a shared anticipation among the monks. The past two days of silence had been transformative. He could feel it in himself and see it in the calm, focused presence of those around him.

The Swami took his place at the front of the hall, his serene expression reflecting the quiet strength of their practice. After a long pause, he began to speak, his voice carrying the weight of experience and wisdom.

"You have all done well. This practice is not easy, but it is powerful. Silence teaches us to observe the ways in which we live outside of ourselves, constantly seeking approval, validation, or a sense of belonging from others."

Harrison nodded inwardly, the truth of the Swami's words resonating deeply. He had spent much of his life striving to impress others, to feel valued through their approval. The silence had stripped away that need, revealing the peace that lay beneath.

The Swami continued, his voice calm but firm. "Tomorrow will be our final day of silence, and in the evening, we will come together to celebrate. But before we end this practice, I want to share an important teaching. One that bridges the gap between silence and speech. This is the practice of skilful speech."

Harrison's curiosity was heightened. He leaned forward slightly, eager to absorb the lesson.

"Speech is one of the most powerful tools we have," the Swami explained. "It can create harmony or division, peace or conflict, understanding or confusion. Too often, we use it without thought, letting it flow from habits and emotions rather than intention. Skilful speech is a practice, a skill to be learned and mastered. It can transform your life and the lives of those around you."

The Swami paused, letting his words sink in.

"There are four main types of speech to avoid. Reflect on these, observe them in your own life, and consider their effects on yourself and others."

The Four Types of Unskilful Speech

False Speech: "To knowingly speak what is not true. This is false speech," the Swami began. "It creates mistrust, confusion, and suffering. Even small lies weaken the fabric of trust that binds us together. False speech actively creates negative karma in your life and in the lives of others around you. Practice speaking only the truth, with care and integrity."

Harrison thought of times when he had exaggerated or bent the truth to impress others. He realised how unnecessary it often was, and how much simpler life could be when grounded in honesty. He felt inspired by how much integrity his words would carry.

Slanderous Speech: "Speech intended to create enmity and division. This is slanderous speech," the Swami continued. "It sows discord and breaks relationships. Be mindful of your words, and use them to foster connection, not separation."

Harrison reflected on casual gossip he had engaged in, not realising the subtle harm it could cause. The idea of using speech to build harmony struck him as both profound and practical.

Harsh Speech: "Speech uttered in anger, intended to cause pain. This is harsh speech. It leaves wounds that may take years to heal. Speak with kindness, even in difficult moments. Let your words be a balm, not a blade."

Harrison felt a pang of guilt as he recalled times he had lashed out in frustration, hurting those he cared about. The concept of speaking with compassion resonated deeply.

Idle Chatter: "Pointless talk that lacks depth or purpose—this is idle chatter. It distracts the mind, wastes time, and adds nothing of value. This is the least critical as it doesn't create bad karma but its still unnecessary, speak with intention, and let your words carry meaning."

Harrison chuckled inwardly, thinking of the countless hours he had spent on social media, engaging in conversations that often led nowhere. The idea of treating speech as a meaningful act felt revolutionary.

A Commitment to Practice

Swami's words left a profound impression on Harrison. He had always thought of speech as something natural, automatic, even trivial. But now he saw it as a skill, one that could shape his relationships, his environment, and even his inner peace. He felt incredibly inspired.

Harrison (to himself): “If I can learn to speak skilfully, to use my words with purpose and kindness, the impact could be enormous. It’s not just about avoiding harm—it’s about creating something positive.”

The Swami concluded the evening with a final piece of advice.

"Speech is like fire. It can warm and illuminate, or it can burn and destroy. Use it wisely. And remember, the foundation of skilful speech is awareness. Observe your words, your intentions, and their effects. This is the beginning of mastery."

The Promise of Celebration

As the monks filed out of the hall, Harrison felt a sense of anticipation for the next day. The silence had been both a challenge and a gift, and he looked forward to celebrating with his companions.

But more than that, he felt a deep commitment to the practice of skilful speech. The lesson was simple but powerful, and he knew it was something he would carry with him far beyond the walls of the monastery.

That night, as he lay on his bed, he reflected on the journey so far. Each day had brought new insights, new challenges, and new growth. And as he drifted off to sleep, he felt an overwhelming sense of gratitude for the path he was on, and for the teachers who were guiding him toward a life of peace and purpose.

Chapter Thirty One

The Final Day of Silence

The fourth and final day of silence unfolded with a serene energy that felt vastly different from the first day. At the beginning of the four days, Harrison had felt separate from the other monks, isolated in his own thoughts and experiences. But now, he realised the silence wasn't about separation; it was about connection.

Without the need for idle chatter, the monastery functioned seamlessly. Each monk moved with purpose, their actions in perfect harmony with one another. He noticed how much more in tune he felt with the group, even without speaking.

"It's not about being alone," he thought to himself. "It's about being part of something greater without the need to fill the space with unnecessary noise."

This realisation brought him a deep sense of peace, and as the sun began to set, he made his way to the great hall, eager for the evening's gathering.

The room buzzed with a quiet anticipation. For four days, they had refrained from speaking, and the Swami now promised a special meditation to mark the end of their silence. He stood at the front of the hall, his eyes warm with encouragement.

"Tonight, we will practise sound meditation," the Swami began. "For the next half hour, you may make any sound you wish. No words, but any other sound. Let these sounds flow naturally from within you. Move if you like, let your body express itself, and embrace this moment of freedom. Let us begin."

The monks closed their eyes, the room plunging into silence once more. Harrison sat still, unsure of how to start. What sound should he make? What if it didn't feel right?

Then, a deep, resonant whale call echoed through the room. It was hauntingly beautiful but also fun. It brought a broad smile to his face, and he felt a spark of inspiration. Moments later, a wolf's howl joined in, followed by a cacophony of sounds, chirps, hums, growls, and shrieks.

Suddenly, Harrison felt a surge of energy. Without thinking, he let out a joyful "LLLAAAA" that burst from his lungs. It felt raw and liberating. Emboldened, he began to beat his chest and make monkey sounds, the rhythm of his movements connecting him to something primal and joyful. Other monkeys responded.

The room was alive with sound. Each monk seemed to be expressing something deeply personal yet universal. Harrison found himself swept up in the energy, his laughter bubbling to the surface as he listened to the absurdity and beauty of the noises around him. Soon, his laughter became uncontrollable, a pure and joyful expression that spread like wildfire through the hall.

One by one, the monks began to laugh. The room filled with the sound of unrestrained joy, each person feeding off the laughter of the others. Harrison had never laughed so freely, so fully. Each time his laughter began to subside, another monk's hysterical giggle would reignite it.

The laughter was infectious, echoing off the walls and reverberating through the hearts of everyone present. For five, ten, fifteen, then twenty minutes, the laughter continued. The room was a symphony of joy, a shared release that transcended words. He had never let go like this before, lost to the pure joy and shared emotion of the monastery.

As the laughter began to fade, the Swami gently played a singing bowl, its clear tone growing slowly and calming the lingering giggles. The monks gradually quieted, their breaths slowing as they transitioned back into stillness.

"Now, lie down and rest in shavasana," the Swami instructed softly.

Harrison stretched out on the cool floor, his body tingling with the aftereffects of laughter and movement. As he closed his eyes, he felt a profound sense of relaxation and gratitude. The sound meditation had been unlike anything he'd ever experienced, a celebration of freedom, connection, and the sheer joy of being alive.

When he awoke, the room was alive with quiet chatter. The silence had ended, but the energy was different now. Conversations were slower, more deliberate. There was no rush, no need to fill the space.

Harrison noticed how much he had changed in just four days. He found himself choosing his words carefully, speaking only when necessary, and often communicating through gestures and expressions rather than speech. The other monks seemed to be doing the same, their words imbued with a sense of intention and peace.

As he walked through the monastery that evening, he felt a deep connection to everyone around him. The silence had stripped away the layers of ego and pretence, leaving behind a shared sense of understanding and unity.

That night, as Harrison sat on the steps of the monastery, gazing at the starry sky, he reflected on the lessons of the past four days. He had learned so much—about himself, about others, and about the power of silence. But most importantly, he had experienced the joy of simply being, unencumbered by the need to impress, to judge, or to speak.

"Words are powerful," he thought to himself, "but so is the absence of them. Silence has taught me to listen to myself, to others, and to the world around me."

The celebration had been perfect, not just for its joyful chaos but for the way it reminded him of the importance of balance. Silence and sound, stillness and movement, solitude and connection—all were part of the same beautiful whole.

As he prepared for the days ahead, he felt ready to carry these lessons with him, knowing they would shape not just his time at the monastery but the rest of his life.

Chapter Thirty Two

Settling into Monastery Life

Over the next few weeks, Harrison truly became a part of the monastery. The laughter and joy from the sound meditation had left a lasting impression on everyone, creating a lighter, more playful atmosphere. Harrison found himself smiling more, connecting with others effortlessly, and embracing the simplicity of life in the mountains.

Each day began with the familiar rhythm of asanas, breathwork, and the unbroken daily practice. His focus and concentration deepened with every session. His mind no longer wandered as it once had. Instead, it stayed steady, rooted in the present moment. He noticed that the stable inner peace he had glimpsed during his early days at the monastery had become a constant presence—a quiet, unwavering foundation within him.

The community of monks played a vital role in this transformation. Their shared commitment to the same understanding, the same practice, created an environment where inner peace felt natural, almost inevitable. Harrison realised how much easier it was to maintain this state of being when surrounded by like-minded individuals, each supporting the other's journey.

As the final week of his stay approached, Harrison felt a growing sense of readiness to take what he had learned and share it with the world. The understanding he had cultivated was so simple, so clear. It wasn't something to be achieved or grasped; it was something to be remembered, to be returned to again and again.

He felt a deep gratitude for the monks, for their wisdom, and for the space they had created for his growth. At the same time, he knew it was time to bring this understanding back into the world, to help others discover the peace that lay within them.

Chapter Thirty Three

A Day with the Swami

At the start of his final week, the Swami approached him with a serene smile.

"You have come far on this journey," he said. "Your focus and peace are steady now, like a flame protected from the wind. As your time here comes to an end, I wish to spend the day with you and teach you the final lesson."

Harrison felt a mix of anticipation and humility. He had learned so much already; what more could there be to understand? Yet he trusted the Swami and knew that whatever the final lesson was, it would be incredibly important.

The morning began with a shared breakfast, simple but filled with gratitude. The Swami ate in silence, savouring each bite with the same mindful presence he brought to every aspect of his life. Harrison followed his example, enjoying each mouthful of food, his appreciation still growing, still developing with each meal.

After breakfast, they set out together, walking slowly through the monastery grounds. The Swami led him to a quiet spot overlooking the valley, where the morning mist hung low over the mountains. They sat side by side, the only sounds the gentle wind as it flowed across the mountain.

As they sat together overlooking the valley, Harrison felt a calm anticipation. He knew this would be the culmination of everything he had learned at the monastery—a final insight to carry with him into the world.

The Swami turned to him, his gaze steady and warm. "Through your time here, tell me: Have you realised who you truly are? And just as importantly, who you are not?"

Harrison took a deep breath, pausing to reflect on the question. His time at the monastery had brought countless revelations, but this question felt like the thread tying them all together.

"In my direct experience, I've realised I am not the mind, nor the body," Harrison said. "These are things I can observe, and because I can observe them, they cannot be who I truly am."

The Swami nodded encouragingly, and Harrison continued.

"What I truly am is the watcher—the one who observes. I am the awareness that sees the thoughts of the mind, feels the sensations of the body. But it's more than that. I've also felt that I am not just an individual. I am part of this life, part of this world. There's a connection to everything. It feels vast, like I'm part of the whole."

The Swami's face lit up with a smile, his approval evident. "Your observation is clear and profound. You have touched the essence of what we teach. The watcher, this awareness, is your concrete self. This is the part of you that observes, the foundation of your practice, that we observe and build skilfully in meditation and also life when we are conscious. But as you've rightly noted, there is also the greater self, the one that connects to all of life. This understanding will deepen and blossom as you walk your path. It is a beautiful unfolding, one that cannot be rushed but will grow with time and practice."

Harrison felt a wave of gratitude wash over him. These words gave structure to the understanding he had been cultivating, grounding the profound experiences of the past weeks.

Finding Sukha

"It's important we address your greatest goal in life and clarify your understanding completely," the Swami said. "Without clarity, there is confusion. When we first met, you believed you were chasing happiness—craving the fleeting joy that external objects provide. What you were actually pursuing was preya, a transient pleasure. But transient pleasures cannot bring lasting happiness."

The Swami paused, his eyes meeting Harrison's. "Tell me, Harrison, what have you achieved here regarding happiness?"

Harrison considered the question carefully. "It feels... different, yet incredibly special. But it's also so simple. I feel this profound sense of peace, ease, and joy. It's not something I chase anymore—it's something that exists as a constant background to my experience. It's hard to put into words, but it's like a lasting happiness and contentment."

"What you're describing is Sukha," the Swami explained, "an authentic state of happiness and ease within a being, one that is lasting."

The Swami paused, letting the weight of his words settle over Harrison.

"Wow. Sukha," Harrison repeated thoughtfully. "I can see how important it is to clarify this—and how learning a new word can completely shift our understanding. 'Happiness' is a wonderful word, but it's so overused and often misunderstood. People confuse it with the feeling of being happy, so it's easy to believe that the things which make you happy will bring happiness. But Sukha... it has nothing to do with external objects."

Harrison pulled out his notebook and turned to a fresh page. At the top, he wrote:

"Sukha: An authentic state of happiness and ease within a being that is lasting."

The Double Meaning of Responsibility

The Swami and Harrison sat silently for a few moments as they enjoyed the stillness.

"Now, let us turn to the final lesson: responsibility."

Harrison's curiosity grew even deeper. Responsibility had always seemed like a mundane word, tied to obligations and duties. What could it mean here, in the context of inner peace?

"Responsibility has a double meaning," the Swami explained. "The first is this: Through your practice, you have learned to consciously observe your experience as the watcher. This means that in any moment, in any situation, you have the ability to choose how to respond. You can react unconsciously, or you can respond consciously. This is the next stage of your training—to consciously respond to life."

Harrison nodded, his thoughts turning to moments where he had reacted in frustration or fear. The idea of responding consciously felt like a powerful shift, one that aligned perfectly with what he had been practising.

"This, too, is a skill," the Swami continued. "It will grow with practice, but it requires vigilance and awareness. In every moment, consciously observe: Am I reacting, or am I responding? Each time you choose to respond, you strengthen this skill and bring greater peace to yourself and those around you."

Harrison felt a deep resonance with these words. It was as though a missing puzzle piece had fallen into place, completing the picture of what he had been learning.

The Swami continued, his tone growing more serious.

"The second meaning of responsibility is this: You are one hundred per cent responsible for your experience in life. You must take responsibility for yourself, for your own inner peace; no longer must you blame others for how you feel. Your daily practice is now your responsibility. Can you commit to this? Can you promise never to break it?"

Harrison didn't hesitate. "Yes, absolutely. I will never miss a day."

The Swami smiled but pressed further. "The knowledge is within you now. But it must be nourished through practice. Without practice, even the greatest insights will fade. So let me ask you—what could happen that might cause you to miss your practice?"

Harrison paused, thinking carefully. "Perhaps an emergency? If I were woken in the night and spent the whole day at the hospital, for example, I might not find the time."

The Swami paused and smiled, his voice firm but compassionate. "Are you saying that on this day, you would have no time to eat? To sleep?"

"No, of course not. I would make time for those."

The Swami's expression softened, but his words carried weight. "Then understand this: Your practice must come before food, before sleep, before anything else. I am not saying you should neglect the emergency. Tend to what needs tending, but know that after the storm calms, before you eat or rest, you must fix yourself. Especially on such a busy day, you need your practice the most, don't you?"

Harrison sat back, stunned by the clarity and simplicity of the Swami's words. It was a profound shift in perspective. His inner peace, his happiness, was his greatest goal in life. So why had he not prioritised it in this way before?

He felt a renewed sense of purpose. This wasn't just a lesson; it was a call to action, a commitment to himself.

"My practice is my foundation," he thought to himself. "No matter what happens in life, I must maintain it. Not out of obligation, but because it is the source of my peace, my clarity, my joy."

The Swami's voice softened, carrying a final note of encouragement. "The knowledge is inside you now. Your role is to cultivate it, to strengthen it through practice. Don't let it become a habit to do unconsciously. Each day, perfect it a little more. This is your responsibility and your freedom. You are ready."

Harrison bowed his head, gratitude welling up inside him. This lesson was not the end of his journey. It was the beginning of a new chapter, one where he carried the monastery's teachings into the world and lived them fully.

As the sun dipped below the mountains, he felt a quiet confidence settle over him. He was ready to take responsibility for his inner peace, for his life, and for the impact he would have on the world.

Clarifying the Lessons

That evening, Harrison sat with the Swami one last time in the library's soft light.

"Swami, I feel like I've learned so much," Harrison said. "But there's so much to remember. How can I hold on to all of this? How can I apply it when life gets overwhelming?"

"Focus on two things: your daily practice and a concise understanding of reality," the Swami replied. "Your practice is your anchor. Never let it falter. The second is your understanding of reality: desires, the watcher, non-suffering, and responsibility."

Harrison nodded thoughtfully. "With desires: I am seeking Sukha, all I want is to feel good inside, so when I feel the pull of desires, I will just respond by feeling good, content and at peace. I will continue to develop my understanding that I am the watcher through meditation and conscious action. With suffering, I now know it is a choice—when I am consciously aware enough to respond, I will not choose to suffer, and when I observe myself suffering, I will let it go. I can respond consciously in every situation, but I know this is a huge challenge, so I will grow this skill each day."

"Beautifully said," the Swami smiled. "Remember these, and you will navigate life with clarity and peace. As you have said, being consciously in control the whole day is the goal, but always be gentle, grow this with practice."

As Harrison left the library, he felt prepared—not because he had all the answers, but because he had the tools to find them within himself.

As the sun dipped below the horizon, he stepped into the cool evening air, ready to embrace the next chapter of his journey with a heart full of gratitude and a mind clear with purpose.

Chapter Thirty Four

The Farewell

Harrison awoke on his final day at the monastery to the soft golden light of dawn spilling through his window. There was a stillness in the air, a sense of quiet reverence that felt different from any other morning. Today was his departure, and yet, it felt less like an ending and more like the beginning of something vast and uncharted.

When he entered the great hall for his morning practice, he was greeted by Kiran and the other monks, who had prepared a special ceremony for him. Each monk held a single flower—bright, delicate, and vibrant. Together, these flowers would form a garland, a symbol of connection, impermanence, and beauty.

He was lost for words, so surprised to be at the centre of attention of such an amazing group. Kiran handed him a small woven mat and gestured for him to sit cross-legged in the centre of the hall. The monks formed a wide circle around him, their robes creating a sea of saffron and ochre.

One by one, each monk approached Harrison. They moved with quiet grace, bowing deeply before him, holding his gaze for a brief but powerful moment, and placing their flower in the growing garland before him. There were no words spoken, yet each look, each flower, carried an unspoken message of gratitude, love, respect, and an unshakeable connection.

As the garland grew, so did Harrison's emotions. He felt his chest tighten, his breath catching as wave after wave of gratitude washed over him. Each flower felt like a thread, weaving him forever into the fabric of this community.

When Kiran approached with the penultimate flower, his warm smile and kind eyes met Harrison's tear-filled gaze. Without hesitation, Harrison let the tears flow, tears of love, of gratitude, of release. They poured down his face, and instead of holding them back, he embraced them. It was not sadness but a profound joy that felt as pure and unfiltered as the laughter he had experienced during the sound meditation.

Finally, the Swami stood. The hall seemed to hold its breath. With slow, deliberate steps, the Swami approached Harrison, carrying the final flower. He bowed deeply, met Harrison's eyes, and placed the last bloom with great care. Then, with quiet reverence, he lifted the garland and placed it over Harrison's head.

The fragrance of the flowers filled his senses, and the weight of the garland felt both light and significant, a reminder of everything he had learned, everything he was carrying forward.

The monks closed their eyes, and together they sat in stillness. Time seemed to dissolve. There was no rush, no need to move. Just a deep, shared presence that bound them together in a way words could never capture.

The Descent

The Swami and Kiran gently guided Harrison to the top of the wide stone steps overlooking the mountain path that would lead him back to the world. The valley stretched out before them, painted in hues of gold and green as the morning sun climbed higher into the sky.

The Swami spoke, his voice calm and clear. "Your journey back down the mountain, you must do alone. You are now responsible for your experience. For carrying this practice, this understanding, into your life. But know this, Harrison: You are never truly alone. We will always be with you, and you with us. Connection transcends distance."

Harrison felt the weight of these words settle deep within him. This was no ordinary farewell; it was a blessing, a call to action, and a promise.

Kiran stepped forward and embraced him tightly. "Remember, my friend, every moment is brand new, an opportunity to begin again. Take it slow, and enjoy every step of the way."

Finally, the Swami placed a gentle hand on Harrison's shoulder, his eyes filled with warmth and trust. They exchanged a final bow, forehead to forehead, a gesture of profound respect and connection.

With a deep breath, Harrison turned and faced the steps. His backpack felt light on his shoulders, but the lessons he carried within him were weightless and eternal.

As he descended the first step, he resisted the urge to look back. He didn't need to; he could feel them with him. The monastery, the Swami, Kiran, and every monk would remain a part of him, woven into the very fabric of his being.

With each step, the world grew larger around him. The path stretched out, winding down through the snow-dusted trees and back toward the distant hum of life below.

But Harrison walked with a stillness inside him, a peace that felt unshakeable. He carried the silence, the laughter, the lessons, and the love with every step he took.

The world awaited him, not as a challenge to conquer, but as a space to practise, to grow, and to share. He was ready.

Chapter Thirty Five

Returning to the World

As Harrison stepped off the plane at Heathrow Airport, the familiar sights and sounds of London greeted him. The chatter of travellers, the hum of announcements, the rush of movement—all the things that once felt overwhelming now seemed manageable. He also noticed a change in how he interacted with people and the world. His awareness was steady, like a calm current running beneath the surface of his experience. His calm presence allowed others to slow down, his smile and kindness touching those he came into contact with. He wasn't perfect. Distractions came and went, but he knew how to return to his inner peace. It was a comforting thought; he had the tools and understanding now, no matter where life led.

The tube journey back home was the first real test. Packed carriages, hurried commuters, and the usual delays could have easily triggered his old frustrations. But this time, he observed the rhythm of it all, the ebb and flow of people, the small acts of kindness, the quiet moments between stations. He thought back to his time on the Indian railway, standing in crowded compartments, feeling a sense of unity rather than stress. If he could find peace there, why not here?

By the time he arrived home, he felt a quiet pride. The tube journey, once a source of tension, had become an enjoyable experience. If he could maintain this state in London, he could maintain it anywhere.

He knew his greatest challenge lay ahead: transitioning from the simplicity of a monk's life back into the busy, bustling reality of the modern world. Before he could share his newfound understanding with others, he needed to prove to himself that he could live and thrive in this environment while maintaining his inner peace.

The First Week

He spent the first week diving fully into life. He reconnected with friends and family, returning to the joyful and busy social life he had always loved. He took on work projects with his usual energy and drive, but with a difference—each day, he started with his morning practice.

Every morning, he woke early, unrolling his mat facing the morning sun. Through his asanas, he felt his body open and his mind settle. Breath by breath, he reconnected with the peace within himself, strengthening his focus and concentration. He journaled after his practice, reflecting on his desires, understanding that he was seeking sukha, each one was a desire to feel good inside and so resolving that whenever his desires arose, to channel their energy toward maintaining his inner peace.

This journalling became a cornerstone of his routine. Each morning, he examined his desires, identity, exploring what was real, slowly deepening his understanding of life and setting intentions for how he would respond to the challenges of the day. Each evening, he reflected on how he had lived, noting where he had succeeded and where he could improve. This cycle of intention and reflection deepened his understanding and solidified his practice.

Building a Support System

Harrison also sought out community, recognising the power of like-minded individuals in supporting his growth. He had always understood you are the product of the people you spend your time with and so made sure he had some people in his life whom he could learn from and also chat to. He joined the yoga centre, where the classes helped him connect with his body and further develop his breath work. He also became a regular with the monks in the park where he could meditate with others and engage in discussions about mindfulness and awareness.

Surrounding himself with people who shared his values and understanding made it easier to stay on track. The camaraderie reminded him of the monastery, where the collective effort of the monks had created an environment of peace and growth.

Forty Days of Integration

As the days turned into weeks, Harrison began to feel more confident. He saw how his new understanding could work in the fast-paced, often chaotic world of the West. Life wasn't without its challenges; there were moments of frustration, emotion, and even doubt. But with his concise understanding and daily practice, he was able to navigate these moments skilfully.

After forty days, he realised he had reached a turning point. The skills and insights he had gained in the monastery were not just surviving, they were thriving in his everyday life. His inner peace was no longer something fragile or fleeting; it was a steady foundation upon which he could build his life.

One morning, as he sat with his journal, Harrison felt a deep sense of readiness. The time had come to share his journey, to help others discover the simplicity and power of inner peace. He opened his notebook to a fresh page, titled it "Seeking Sukha" and began to write.

As the words flowed, he felt a deep gratitude for the journey that had brought him to this point. From the hustle of his old life to the quiet stillness of the monastery, every experience had been a step on the path. Now, he was ready to share that path with the world.

With each sentence, he felt the joy of creation, the thrill of sharing something meaningful. His book was not just a story—it was a guide, a beacon for anyone seeking peace in the midst of life's chaos. And as he wrote, he knew with certainty that this was the work he was meant to do...

What's Next?

Making the Most of Your Journey

To fully integrate the teachings from this book into your life, consider following these steps:

1. I recommend you read this book and take notes, then journal on the lessons and insights you gained. When we journal we translate new information into our own understanding.

2. Our minds naturally retain only a small percentage of what we read—Its really important to understand how your mind works, you can not remember word for word a whole book. Even 10 percent of it is 20 pages. So lets say you remember 1% that's two pages and is more realistic. So you need to condense the book down to that 1% condense down the points you want to remember. Then just learn that.

3. Develop your own daily practice - Use the practice I shared in this book. Or check out all the other great ones I share too. Don't hesitate to message me and I will send you one.

Continuing Your Journey

If Harrison's story has resonated with you and you'd like to deepen your practice, I offer several ways to support your journey:

- Free Courses: Regular workshops focused on developing effective habits for a fulfilling life

- "Master Your Mind and Develop Inner Peace": A comprehensive course with me that guides you step by step through the process of developing lasting inner peace

- Additional Resources: Tools and guidance to support your ongoing practice

To learn more about these opportunities and access additional resources, visit: www.duncanstarrboltt.com

Remember, like Harrison, you're not just reading a book—you're beginning a journey of transformation.

SCAN ME

About the Author

Duncan Starr-Boltt is a happiness and inner peace coach who bridges the gap between high achievement and contentment. As a world record holder and former business owner, he understands firsthand the challenges of finding balance in a success-driven world.

For over twenty years, Duncan has delved deep into the study of happiness and inner peace, exploring everything from mindfulness and yoga to Buddhism and modern coaching techniques. His journey has taken him to India, where he spent time studying studying yoga, meditation and more. His unique perspective comes from combining Eastern wisdom with Western understanding—having grown up discussing neuroscience with his father, a brain expert, while also immersing himself in the ancient practices of yoga and meditation.

Drawing from his twelve years of running a successful gym and working as a personal trainer, Duncan witnessed how many high achievers struggled to find peace outside their work. This observation, coupled with his own experience of being unable to relax despite outward success, led him on a journey to discover a simpler, more effective approach to happiness.

"In the West, we often try to fix the mind," Duncan explains. "In the East, they teach you that you are not the mind. This simple shift in perspective changes everything."

Today, Duncan divides his time between the peaceful shores of Crete, where he lives with his wife and their golden retriever,

Louie, and summers in Cambridge. Through his coaching and writing, he helps others discover that lasting peace and success can coexist harmoniously.

This book shares not only the practical tools and insights gained from his journey but also the transformative experiences that shaped his understanding of true happiness.

Printed in Great Britain
by Amazon

59008043R00126